"Finally! Someone has had the cleverness, initiative, and imagination to set down on paper a film language that has been passed down and amalgamated only by word of mouth since the days of Méliès and D. W. Griffith. Like Dr. Johnson's *Dictionary of the English Language*, Christopher Kenworthy's *Master Shots* series seeks to make tangible and permanent what otherwise might be gone with the wind."

— John Badham, Director, *Saturday Night Fever, WarGames, Short Circuit*; Author, *I'll Be in My Trailer* and *John Badham on Directing*; Professor of Media Arts, The Dodge School, Chapman University

"I've directed five features and a ton of TV and I wish to God I'd had this book at the beginning of my career. It's an unbelievably comprehensive resource for filmmakers. I can't wait to go back and look at Volumes 1 and 2."

— Tom Lazarus, Screenwriter, Director, Educator, Author, *The Last Word*

"You can take ten years to figure out lensing or you can read this book and use that ten years to create your art instead. Your choice."

— Tony Levelle, Author, *Digital Video Secrets*; Co-author, *Producing with Passion*

"The latest installment in Kenworthy's *Master Shots* series lives up to its predecessors and then some, offering up even more exciting ways to frame and follow your action. All three *Master Shots* books belong on the bookshelf of every serious filmmaker."

— Troy DeVolld, Author, *Reality TV*

"Christopher Kenworthy's *Master Shots V*[...] for both directors and cameramen, and [...] works in or studies the art of filmmaking. [...] instructive with great visual samples."

— Catherine Ann Jones, Author, *The Way of Story* and *Heal Your Self with Writing*; Screenwriter and TV Writer, *Touched by an Angel* and *The Christmas Wife*

"Christopher Kenworthy teaches readers the nouns and verbs and participles and definite articles of the language of cinema, equipping them to tell stories on the screen with the power that flows from fluency. Kenworthy understands the interplay between image, character, story, and emotion. He writes so that his readers will understand, too."

— Chris Riley, Author, *Hollywood Standard, 2nd Edition*

"*Master Shots Vol 3* continues this ultimate reference-book series that is a must-have guide for directors and cinematographers on how to find interesting ways to tell your story visually."

— Marx H. Pyle, Producer/Co-host, GenreTainment; Director/Creator, Reality On Demand

"A fascinating look at amazingly simple ways to use the camera, making this an essential read for anyone looking to hone the craft of visual storytelling."

— Erin Corrado, www.onemoviefiveviews.com

"*Master Shots Vol 3* offers fabulous insight into the purpose behind each shot. I'm so thankful for this book — it's my new secret weapon!"

— Trevor Mayes, Screenwriter/Director

CHRISTOPHER KENWORTHY

MASTER SHOTS VOL 3

THE DIRECTOR'S VISION 100 Setups, Scenes and Moves for Your Breakthrough Movie

MICHAEL WIESE PRODUCTIONS

Published by Michael Wiese Productions
12400 Ventura Blvd. #1111
Studio City, CA 91604
(818) 379-8799, (818) 986-3408 (FAX)
mw@mwp.com
www.mwp.com

Cover design by Johnny Ink. www.johnnyink.com
Edited by Gary Sunshine
Interior design by William Morosi
Printed by McNaughton & Gunn

Manufactured in the United States of America

Library of Congress Cataloging-in-Publication Data

Kenworthy, Christopher.
 Master shots. Volume 3, The director's vision : 100 setups, scenes, and moves for your
breakthrough movie / Christopher Kenworthy.
     pages cm
 ISBN 978-1-61593-154-5
 1. Cinematography. I. Title. II. Title: Director's vision.
 TR850.K4633 2013
 777'.8--dc23
                              2013015076

Printed on Recycled Stock

CONTENTS

INTRODUCTION

Nothing is more important than learning to see like a director, and readers tell me that the *Master Shots* books give them that ability. They learn to shoot like pros. They learn to make a low-budget shot look like it cost a fortune. They find ways to be inventive, when the clock is ticking.

My readers have asked for more. I received many emails asking for a third book, one that goes deeper, showing more than a collection of moves. People didn't want me to show another 100 cool shots. They wanted to learn how to develop a director's vision.

The best movies need great acting, a fabulous script, and an adaptable crew. They also need great shots. Without creative camera work, you're letting down everybody else, watering down the story and wasting the opportunity to make a great film.

If you shoot a great actor in an average way, the result is disappointing. If you shoot an exquisite set without innovation, the money's been thrown away. If you shoot a wonderful story with traditional setups, the result will be boring. If you care about your film, you should care about every shot. Masterful shots are your gift to the audience.

Your job is not to look cool by creating exciting camera setups, nor is your job to shoot basic coverage and hope

the editor can save your movie. Your job is to design shots that reveal story, expose emotion, explore character, and capture the unique feeling of your film. At the same time, you should stamp your film with your own style. This book can help you do that.

Almost every day I get emails from people who are using the *Master Shots* books. I am told by experienced directors, teachers, film school students, and commercial videomakers that these are the books they take to set with them. These are the books they use to solve problems, and the books they have in hand when they first sit down to imagine how they're going to shoot their film.

Writers tell me they have gained a better understanding of how scenes work, having read my books, and they can now write in ways that make scripts appealing to directors. They understand the flow of movement and emotion that is the key to the *Master Shots* approach.

Actors and drama teachers tell me the *Master Shots* books are one of the best ways for performers to get to grips with the needs of the camera. With the tools in these books explained to them, actors better understand how directors see the world, and know what they are trying to achieve.

Master Shots Vol 1 is the best introduction to powerful camera moves that can be applied to your movie. It's a crash course in camera work that can be applied to just about any scene. It's used by absolute beginners, along with directors who have been working in Hollywood for decades.

Master Shots Vol 2 shows how to solve the director's greatest challenge: keeping a film visually interesting when then action stops and the talking begins. I get many emails from directors telling me that their films have been brought to life by seeing the importance of capturing dialogue well. *Master Shots Vol 2* is for directors who are serious about getting to the heart of their films. It's also the most popular book with actors, because it shows how to make their most important dialogue scenes shine.

When directors need to solve a problem, they dip into the books and find a solution. If the exact shot they want isn't there, they combine two or three ideas to create something new. They also study each book before they get to set, reading it from cover to cover, learning the moves and getting a feel for this way of seeing. This means they have ideas in mind, but are flexible enough to adapt on-set.

Master Shots Vol 3 takes this all a step further. It can help you stand out from the crowd, by showing you how to get to the core of a scene and bring its meaning to the screen clearly, effectively, and with style. You will find your vision, and discover how you can realize it cinematically.

The shots in this book were chosen as pure, clear examples of innovative and precise technique. I watched hundreds of films, and found those with camera moves that achieve five key goals: They reveal character, they tell the story, they look like they are expensive, they are easy to achieve, and, most importantly, every shot was chosen to be adaptable. Every shot is something you can make your own, whatever your budget. In most cases, the shots can be achieved with the minimum of equipment, and the adventurous can adapt them to a handheld camera, or get them working with a cheap stabilizer. A few require you to cover for safety issues, and will work better if you have access to a good dolly and crane. The equipment isn't important. Once you learn to see like a director, you will find a way to get the shot.

I didn't want to present 100 shots you can copy, so much as 100 shots you can use to stamp your own style onto your movie. By the time you've finished this book you will know how you want your films to look, and how you can get that result easily.

This book is more advanced than the other *Master Shots* volumes, because the shots achieve several results at the same time. The move, framing, or angle may be simple, but the effect is profound. This book can still be used by ambitious beginners. If you're new to film, use this book with the other two, to understand how the camera achieves its results. If you've been shooting for years, this book will push you to develop new approaches, combining ideas and creating original shots.

If you own all three books, I recommend that you read all three right through, before you begin shooting. Use *Master Shots Vol 3* to get to the heart of the scene and create the master shot that guides a scene or sequence. *Master Shots Vol 2* should be applied to your dialogue scenes, to make sure you're getting the most out of them. Keep *Master Shots Vol 1* handy for when you need a quick fix or a simple idea to ramp up the action.

For directors and producers, you should make sure other members of the cast and crew have access to the books (or buy them their own copies if the budget allows), so you can all stay on the same page. If everybody knows what sort of shots you're creating, it's easier for all to work together.

It's especially important that your cinematographer have a copy of the books. Some cinematographers are more hands-on than others, and if you're designing all the shots, they find it easier to work with you if they know what approach you're using. Equally, if you're a cinematographer, these books can help you save a director from making a dull movie. You may find your director is more interested in the actors than the camera, so you can use these books to show how the camera can help them.

When directors see that a good performance depends on a creative camera, they take your work more seriously.

In *Master Shots Vol 1*, I aimed to show that moving the camera in creative ways can enliven any scene and contribute to the story. That first volume was a bestseller for years and is used in schools around the world, and by many filmmakers, because the techniques can be applied over and over again.

With *Master Shots Vol 2,* I showed that dialogue is the soul of any film, and needs to be filmed with flair and passion. Both the *Master Shots* books, I am told, accompany directors when they're on-set, on Hollywood TV shows, on movie sets in Australia and on commercial shoots in China.

If those books cover so much ground, is there really a need for a third book?

With *Master Shots Vol 3,* I wanted to show filmmakers an advanced approach to shot design, that inspires a way of seeing. Seeing how other directors have solved problems, revealed story, and captured feelings, you will learn to shoot more inventively.

By the time you have studied the shots in this book, you will never be satisfied with an average setup. You will always try to find a twist, slant, or change of perspective that brings life and purpose to your shots. This book is an advanced text because, whatever your experience, it challenges you to imagine a creative solution for every scene in your film.

This book urges you to imagine. Study the still frames and overhead diagrams, and imagine how the shots could be created. Then, imagine changing one variable — angle, actor position, camera height — and imagine how the scene would change. Finally, imagine how you could do a better job.

The camera is like a blank canvas. The moment you point it at a subject, you begin to tell a story. If you change the camera's height, you tell a different story. Move the camera to a different angle, and you create different emotions. How you position and move the actors in the frame changes how we feel about them. Everything you do counts, so make sure you understand what's going on in the frame, how the lens affects the meaning, and how movement conveys story.

When people start making films they sometimes think it's about pointing the camera at actors and recording a performance. Great directors know that the film is crafted in camera, sculpted and colored by the angles, moves, blocking, and framing that you apply to each shot.

I spend a lot of time on movie sets and I see a lot of wasted opportunities. This is true whether I'm on a low-budget feature, a student film, or even a big-budget movie. Directors miss opportunities all the time, settling for average shots when they could aim for greatness. This has nothing to do with lack of money. It can be made worse by limited time. Usually, though, it is because directors run out of ideas.

When designing shots, whether it's weeks ahead of the shoot during storyboarding, or moments before you roll — think of the story. Where have the characters just been, and where are they trying to get? What does your hero want in this scene, and what is being done about it? Think of these things, and shots will suggest themselves to you.

When you've studied the shots in this book, and seen how directors maneuver through a story with grace, your imagination will ignite.

HOW TO USE THIS BOOK

You can browse through *Master Shots Vol 3* to find a shot that best suits your scene, but if you read the whole book, you will learn the imaginative techniques required to design your own shots.

To appreciate a chapter you need to read the text, while referring to the images. You can then imagine how you could use the shot yourself, and picture how small changes to the shot would affect the result.

Use *Master Shots 3* during preproduction, and then have the book nearby on-set, so that you can find alternative ideas, or add something extra to a scene. Combine several techniques in one scene to create something completely new. Sharing the book with actors can be an excellent way to make them aware of the lens, and how you're capturing their magic.

ABOUT THE IMAGES

Each chapter features frame grabs from popular movies, to show how successfully the specific technique explored has been used before. The overhead shots show how the camera and actors move to achieve this effect. The white arrows show camera movement. The black arrows show actor movement.

The most essential points have been illustrated, but as this is an advanced text, some of the shots are not illustrated. In any given chapter, you may see one shot with an overhead diagram showing how it works. The next shot may not have an overhead diagram. This means you have to do more of the work yourself. You have to look at the shot, read the text, and decode the camera move. This takes some practice, but this is the practice every director needs.

In Chapter Eleven, there are more frame grabs from movies, but no overhead shots. This will further encourage you to imagine how the shots could be achieved. That is the purpose of this book: to get you used to imagining camera moves clearly.

CHAPTER 1

ADVANCED LENSING

LONG LENS DISTANT

A long lens focuses in on your subject, or main character, while revealing the environment around them. This works especially well when the camera is a long way from the actor, and the background is even farther back. In these frames from *The Book of Eli*, the long lens forces everything but the character out of focus, so our concentration is firmly on him and his expression.

Set the camera up a long way from your actor, with other objects or actors much closer to the camera. When you focus on the actor, the foreground objects or actors, as well as the background, are thrown out of focus. Get the foreground actors to cross horizontally in front of the screen to exaggerate the effect.

The actor will not appear to move fast toward the camera, but objects moving across the frame will appear to move quickly. This makes us see the character is trapped or struggling in a chaotic world.

The frames from *Black Swan* show how you can use a long lens to pan with a character, revealing foreground and background elements in the one shot. It's often assumed that you need to start with a wide shot to establish the space, then use medium shots and close-ups on the actors, but a well-planned shot can do all this work for you.

Here, the camera does nothing but follow the character across the room, but by placing actors closer to the camera, as well as actors in the far background, the entire scene is revealed clearly in one shot.

When using a long lens, the background is drawn toward the subject, and the foreground is compressed toward the subject. In this frame from *The Road*, you can see how the foreground and background elements appear closer to the actor than they actually are. By placing the actor to one side of the frame, with the foreground filling the other side of the frame, you create a strong impression of the environment while drawing the viewer's eye to the character.

The Book of Eli. Directed by the Hughes Brothers. Summit Entertainment, 2010.

Black Swan. Directed by Darren Aronofsky. Fox Searchlight Pictures, 2010.

The Road. Directed by John Hillcoat. FilmNation Entertainment, 2009.

LONG LENS CLOSE

You might assume that a long lens is used like a telescope, to get you closer to the action, but it's better if you think of it as a tool that narrows the camera's view of the world. A long lens, when placed close to an actor, shows almost nothing except the actor you're focused on, making it ideal for close-ups and extreme close-ups.

Place your camera close to the actors and use a long lens to focus on the eyes. As you can see with these first two frames from *Hard Candy*, you will need to focus on the eyes. The rest of the face will go slightly out of focus. If possible, ask the actors not to move their faces toward or away from the camera during these shots, or it will be difficult to maintain focus on the eyes. Don't worry about the rest of the face being blurred, because this draws attention to the eyes.

The third frame is not quite as close, but still has the effect of drawing attention to the actor's facial expression. Clothes, hair, and background may be glimpsed, but the camera has been placed so that the emphasis is on the character's facial expression. This works especially well because she is framed right to the edge of the screen, rather than leaving the usual space over her shoulder. In the fourth frame, the same effect is created by framing him hard to the left.

The final frame shows how you can continue this sequence of long lens shots, by being slightly farther back, but shooting from the side. The actor's face is framed even harder to the left, leaving a lot of empty screen space to the right, which can be filled by the actor's hand movements. With the focus on his face, even his hands are slightly out of focus. By drawing our attention so tightly to the actors' faces, a close long lens makes us watch them intently and hang on to their every word.

Hard Candy. Directed by David Slade. Lionsgate, 2006. All rights reserved.

LONG LENS STATIONARY

You can create powerful effects with a long lens without moving the camera during the shot. In these stills from *The Road,* a simple cut between two locked-off shots creates a sense of the characters' struggle through the environment.

In the first shot, the camera is placed a long way back, and a medium-to-long lens is used to show the characters within the environment. The standard approach with a long lens is to make use of foreground, midground, and background, but here they are all blended together. With nothing intruding into the foreground, and the background drawn close to the characters, this shot removes all depth. This creates a sense of stasis, as though all movement is slow and difficult.

The next shot uses a longer lens, closer to the actors, and now the background trees extend out of the frame. This creates a sense of imprisonment, because the characters are moving forward — we can see them walking — but do not appear to get closer to the camera, and the environment now appears to be dwarfing them.

Set up your camera so that when the cut is made, the characters appear to be in exactly the same part of the frame, whatever else is shown. By doing this you create the sense of being trapped, making it difficult to move forward.

The frames from *The Adjustment Bureau* also show that with an extremely long lens you can use focus to reveal new detail. An extremely long lens, placed far back from your actor, will throw the background out of focus. The second actor can then walk into the background as a blur, and the camera is focused on him. This is achieved by pulling focus, not by moving the lens or camera. If your lens is long enough, the foreground actor will become extremely blurred, almost vanishing from the shot. By using extreme defocus, a stationary long lens creates the feeling of a cut without actually cutting, and without moving the camera.

The Road. Directed by John Hillcoat. FilmNation, 2009.

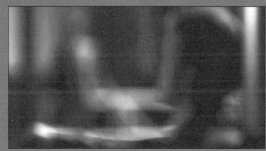

The Adjustment Bureau. Directed by George Nolfi. Universal Pictures, 2011.

LONG LENS IN MOTION

When you use a long lens, all sideways movement of the camera becomes exaggerated, even if it's just a slight wobble. This means the long lens isn't suitable for any camera move where there's potentially a lot of movement, such as a long steadicam shot, or a handheld scene.

This doesn't mean that the long lens should remain stationary. Although there are challenges related to focus and framing, a long lens can be used to create extremely powerful moving shots.

In *Hard Candy*, a simple dolly shot is made more interesting by using a long lens. When pushing in on a character, you normally use a short lens because it speeds up the feeling of the dolly move — things get big and close quickly. By using a long lens, you have to set up more track and push in a lot farther and faster for it to even look like a dolly shot. If you push in over just a few feet, nothing much will change in the frame. So set up your camera a long way back from the character, and then push in over ten feet or more. This will require extremely careful focusing, but don't worry too much if focus slips slightly during the shot, so long as you are focused on the eyes when the camera comes to rest.

If so much track is needed, and if focus is critical, what's the advantage to this sort of shot? The long lens narrows the angle of view, concealing the surrounding environment. This is why it's used for close-ups; it focuses in on the actor. When combined with a dolly it exaggerates this focus on a character.

If you used a short lens, you would end up with a lot of background in the frame, or you would have to get so close to the actor that her face would appear distorted. The long lens also makes it easier to throw the background out of focus, so that actor is isolated in the frame. This effect is ideal for dramatic moments or revelations, such as this one, when we see the character for the first time.

You can achieve another strong effect by keeping the camera in one place, and tracking a fast-moving actor running through a crowded location. This is nothing more than a pan, but the long lens, combined with the actor's movement, creates an impression of extreme speed.

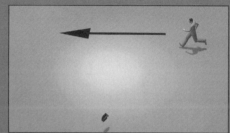

The Adjustment Bureau. Directed by George Nolfi. Universal Pictures, 2011.

Hard Candy. Directed by David Slade. Lionsgate, 2006.

SHORT LENS DISTANT

Short lenses create a sense of space. Often used to show landscapes, they are just as effective at showing a large indoor space. They will make a small room appear larger, and a large space seem cavernous.

In this shot from *The Adjustment Bureau*, a slight dolly to the right increases this sense of space. There is no motion other than the camera dollying to the right, without panning. It's important to have something or somebody roughly in the center of the space, if you want to draw attention to the size of the room. If they are too close to camera, the focus will be entirely on the character, and if they are too far away the sense of space will not be revealed by the sideways motion.

Short lenses also exaggerate movement toward or away from the camera, which means that when your actors move just a short distance away they appear to move rapidly away. This can be used to throw your characters from a seemingly normal space into a wide-open one. In these shots from *Léon: The Professional*, the actors stand outside a doorway in a seemingly dark, enclosed space, but as the camera dollies to the right, they move away from the camera and to the edge of the building.

The camera keeps moving, until the original background (the dark building) is completely out of shot. This creates a fantastic transition between a dark space that feels enclosed, and a huge, expansive city. When the shot begins, we don't know if we're in an alleyway, or other enclosed space, but the camera move reveals the characters to be part of a much bigger world.

This is a useful technique when you want to show the characters making a transition from one place, or one state of mind, to another. The camera move itself is exceptionally simple, dollying to the right as the actors make their move, but it is made effective by lens choice. The short lens creates the necessary movement away from the camera, and the sense of space and landscape beyond and around them.

The Adjustment Bureau. Directed by George Nolfi. Universal Pictures, 2011.

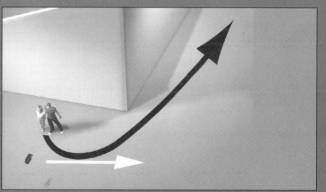

Léon: The Professional. Directed by Luc Besson. Columbia Pictures/Gaumont Film Company, 1994.

SHORT LENS CLOSE

The short lens exaggerates distance, so camera moves seem faster. People move more rapidly toward or away from the camera, and objects can appear distorted.

A small camera move, combined with a strong character move, creates a feeling of urgency. In these frames from *Inception*, we see a wide internal space. The camera pushes forward, but only slightly, as the character moves past the camera and into the room.

The camera move, although small, helps to make this more dynamic than if you only have the actor move. Make sure your actor passes close to the camera to get the greatest sense of movement away from the camera.

The first frame from *A Very Long Engagement* shows how effectively a short lens can be used to increase the presence of an object. The gun, which would have to be extremely close to the lens itself, appears much longer than it would be in real life. This distortion also amplifies its movement, so as the actor moves the gun around slightly, it appears to wobble wildly. This means that we keep our attention on the actor, who is in focus, but remain acutely aware of the gun. It feels as though it's being pointed at us, and creates a more intense sense of danger than if a medium lens was used.

The next shot shows how short lenses distort faces. Whatever's closer to the camera appears closer than it really is; in essence, this means that people appear to have slightly bigger noses than usual. To avoid this being too much of a problem (or a comedic effect), you can angle the camera from above. A slight tilt can also help. By positioning the camera in this way you can obtain the slightly dreamlike feeling of distortion offered by a short lens, without making faces look too unusual.

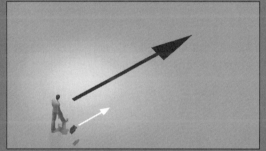

A Very Long Engagement. Directed by Jean-Pierre Jeunet. Warner Independent Pictures, 2004. All rights reserved.

Inception. Directed by Christopher Nolan. Warner Bros. Pictures, 2010. All rights reserved.

SHORT LENS STATIONARY

Traditionally, short lenses are used to show a wide view, whether that's a landscape, or as shown here, a large room. In the frame from *Black Swan* you can see that a short lens doesn't simply capture a wide view, but can exaggerate distances, so that a room appears larger. In this shot, by having somebody on the left close to camera, this effect is enhanced even more.

For more dynamic scenes, however, the stationary short lens can create extremely powerful shots when you let the actors move to fill the space. In this shot from *Schindler's List*, the camera barely moves, only titling up and down to accommodate the actors' heights as they move into shot.

When the scene begins, both are close to camera, but facing different directions. They then begin a sequence of moves, almost like a dance, where one moves away, as another moves forward, constantly rearranging themselves in front of the camera. It is as though the director set up seven different shots from the same position, and then got the actors to play the scene moving between these seven setups.

To get this effect, that is exactly what you should do. Position your camera low to the ground, so you can capture the full length of the characters. Make sure there is a motivation for the characters to kneel near the camera. (In this example, they are looking through old files and papers.) Then find the best six or seven compositions by positioning the actors around the room. When you've found the strongest looks, you can begin to work the story into the scene, connecting the images you've created to the actors' movement. Alternatively, start with the script and let the actors improvise their movement, and find the images that work the best.

What you want to avoid is moving the actors just for the sake of it, or moving them into position artificially. Each movement toward or away from the camera should be motivated by a desire to go somewhere else, look at something else, or talk to another person. When the motivation is clear, this extreme movement toward and away from the camera appears entirely natural, and one lengthy shot feels like an elegant sequence of perfect compositions.

Black Swan. Directed by Darren Aronofsky. Fox Searchlight Pictures, 2010.

Schindler's List. Directed by Steven Spielberg. Universal Pictures, 1993.

SHORT LENS IN MOTION

The tendency for a short lens to exaggerate and increase a sense of movement becomes even more noticeable when the camera moves. A short lens creates a sense of great motion, when the subject stays relatively close to the camera and moves rapidly through the environment.

In the first example, from *The Adjustment Bureau,* the camera is quite close to the running actor, and catches up slightly during the shot. Due to the nature of the short lens, this slight catch-up feels quite extreme, but not as extreme as the surrounding motion. The scenery appears to rush past at an almost supernatural speed, which enhances the speed of the chase. When working outdoors, you might need to use extremely short lenses to create this effect, as the walls, trees, and objects are quite a distance to either side.

When working indoors you can use a short-to-medium lens to achieve the same effect as seen in the frames from *Black Swan*. As Natalie Portman moves forward, the camera remains roughly the same distance from her. The walls, people, and other objects are all close by, and so they appear to rush past, making her movement seem far more rapid than it really is.

At some points in this shot, other actors move toward and past the camera, which adds even more to the effect.

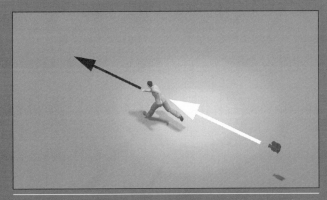

THE MEDIUM LENS

The medium lens, as its name suggests, can lead to quite dull shots. It looks too much like the images we see when looking at the world with our eyes, rather than with a camera. To make the most of it, interesting setups, small moves, and clever framing can make it worth using.

The medium lens is a good choice when you want to see the actors within their environment. You can create scenes where you are aware of the room or space, and the character, without either being emphasized over the other. This is shown in the frames from *Schindler's List* where we see the actors, take in their expressions, and also get a good picture of the room they are in.

To make this shot more interesting, the director started with the camera down low, and turned to follow the actors. The camera comes to rest as they stand briefly, and then pushes in as they take up their final position. With nothing more than a pan and a short dolly move, we effectively get to see three interesting compositions.

As seen in the final frame, from *Black Swan*, the medium lens can also be used to convey a great deal of visual information. The focus is on Natalie Portman in the foreground, but the background (including reflections) has been filled out into the distance so that we see the size of the room, the number of people, and the presence of the piano. A short lens would not let us see the actor within this space, and a long lens would cut out too much of the room. Here, the medium lens lets us see the actor, and her expression, while taking in the scale of the scene.

Black Swan. Directed by Darren Aronofsky. Fox Searchlight Pictures, 2010.

Schindler's List. Directed by Steven Spielberg. Universal Pictures, 1993.

CUTTING THE LENS

There is nothing to stop you shooting with short, medium, and long lenses, then cutting between all those shots. In many films, and especially television, that is exactly what happens. You often begin with a wide lens establishing the scene, move to a medium lens to show two actors, and then switch to a long lens for close-ups.

This is such a standard practice that it's worth thinking about working in other ways. You can shoot an entire scene with a short lens, even though the close-ups will appear distorted. Equally, you can shoot landscapes and establishing shots with a long lens, even though you will cut out a lot of the angle of view. These are quite extreme alternatives that are worth experimenting with.

Whatever you choose, however, take careful note of where you position the camera. You should choose the lens according to the effect you want, then move the camera to get the framing you want.

In these frames from *Love Actually* you can see cuts between various long and medium lenses, but to enhance the effect of the lens change the camera itself is moved closer and further away from the actor. It is, however, kept roughly in line with the center of the bed, to help orient the viewer. If the camera moved all around the room, with lots of lens changes, the cuts would feel quite disorienting.

In *Never Let Me Go,* a relatively long lens frames the couple, then a longer lens frames the single character. When the camera cuts back to the couple an even longer lens has been used, but the camera has been moved around slightly, so we are looking more directly at the actors. As the intensity of the scene increases, it helps to look more directly into the characters' eyes. The cut to a longer lens at this point throws the background out of focus, and therefore puts the focus more strongly on the characters than the space they are in.

There are no rules when it comes to which lenses, or how many different lenses, you should use in a scene, but whatever you choose, don't forget to move the camera, to enhance or reduce the effects of your lens choice.

Never Let Me Go. Directed by Mark Romanek. Fox Searchlight
Pictures, 2010. All rights reserved.

Love Actually. Directed by Richard Curtis. Universal Pictures, 2003.
All rights reserved.

MOTION

BLENDED MOVES

The simplest setups can lead to complex-looking moves. Your aim should never be to look complicated for the sake of impressing people, but sometimes you want to create a great sense of motion and space, without excessive camera moves.

These frames from *Laurel Canyon* show a move that is nothing more than a simple dolly to the right. It is the way that the camera and actors are staged within this framing that makes the shot interesting. This shot establishes the space that they are entering together for the first time, so it has been designed to heighten the sense of the environment seeming new, daunting, and even overwhelming.

This is achieved in several ways. The actors emerge from behind the bushes to the left, and then snake to their left, and away from camera. This motion feels almost like people picking their way through the jungle. This is a subconscious impression, but the shot creates the feeling that they are exploring or finding their way, rather than strolling into a familiar environment.

When they move away from the camera, we get to see the bags they are dragging with them, which emphasizes their arrival more effectively than if we saw them in medium close-up.

As they move away from the camera, they appear to shrink in the frame, while the house and its grounds remain the same size. The characters are effectively swallowed up by the environment, which is made to appear unnerving to them.

The shot also effectively establishes essential aspects of this space for later use in the story, such as the presence of a pool, chairs by the pool, and a house on the hill, and yet it is all achieved with nothing more than a slight motion to the right. When planning your shots, work out what story elements you're trying to bring out of the script, and see if a simple move, combined with characters moving through the scene, can give you everything you need. There's no need to set up ten different shots when one does the job effectively.

Laurel Canyon. Directed by Lisa Cholodenko. Sony Pictures Classics, 2003. All rights reserved.

CAMERA IN MOTION

When you want to create a feeling of extreme speed, during a chase sequence, you need to move the camera at the same speed as the actor. This enables you to keep the character's face in the frame, so we can see his expression, while simultaneously having the environment rush by.

As you can see in these frames from *The Karate Kid*, the camera is set up ahead of the actor, and is angled on to him. It dollies along the same path as he does, remaining the same distance at all times. If you have the actor get closer or farther away from the camera, it can create unexpected results, and can even make it look as though the action is slowing down. Although there are benefits to experimenting with such setups, if you want to create a rapid running scene with no change in pace, then keep the camera at the same angle and distance. Also, adjust the framing throughout so that the actor remains in exactly the same part of the frame.

To get the sense of speed, it's also important to have objects between the actor and the camera. As these flash past, out of focus, they enhance the effect. Having the actor run past a wall is much more effective than if he was running in an open space.

The second set of frames shows a slight variation on this approach, taking even more advantage of objects between the actors and the camera. The camera moves at the same pace as the actors, but a longer lens is used, and we are lower down, so that cars and people obscure the frame even more. This approach should be used when you want the sense of people rushing through a crowded or busy place. It takes only a few cars and people to create the impression of a chase scene through a busy place.

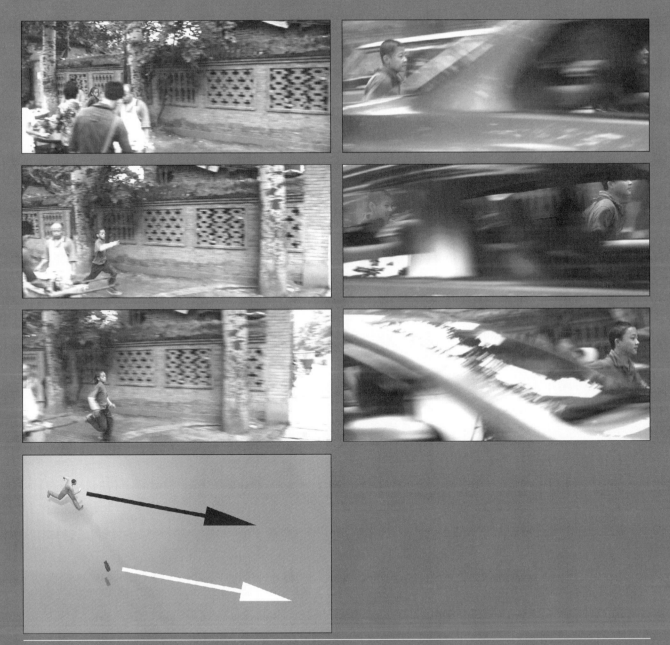

CHARACTER DRIVES CAMERA

When you let the character's motion drive the camera, you help the audience identify with the character. This is particularly useful when there's no dialogue, and you want to convey movement and emotion. It can be difficult to communicate emotion during camera moves, because the actor's face may not be where our attention goes. By letting the actor's movement dictate the shot, you keep the audience focused on what the character is thinking or feeling. Equally, when the camera freezes in place and the character moves away, you can show that a decision has been made.

In these frames from *The Book of Eli,* the shot begins with the camera framed on the broken pipes in the background. This establishes that it's a new scene, but we have no idea whether we'll cut to something else, or push in on the pipes. To have the character walk in from the left is a moment of surprise that draws our attention to her much more strongly than if we'd cut to her already in motion.

The camera then moves with her, by dollying to the right, keeping her at the same position in the frame. The background moves and changes, indicating that she's moving to a new place, but we are able to see her face clearly.

She comes to a stop where the environment changes. Here, the horizontal pipes end, and more broken pipes run off into the distance. This indicates a moment of choice — she could carry on, or head off in a new direction. This would work just as well on a street corner, or at a crossroads of two paths.

As she comes to a halt, so does the camera. To show her indecision, the director has her look back in the direction that she's already come. Then, as she walks away from the camera, it stays where it is, letting her be engulfed by the location.

There are many variations on this setup, but the essential point is that the camera remains stationary unless the character is moving. When you do that, you keep the audience focused on the character's internal monologue. When the character moves in a different direction, and the camera remains stationary, you show that there's been a moment of change or decision.

REVEAL MOVES

When you want to introduce a new character, you can do so by creating a sequence of moves that emphasize their importance. These frames from *Heavenly Creatures* show how the shot begins with the teacher on the left of frame, and then ends with Kate Winslet in almost exactly the same framing. The move replaces one character with another, so that rather than merely appearing in the scene, she takes it over.

By starting with a conventional framing, you lull the viewer into expecting an ordinary sequence of cuts, so it's a surprise when the camera arcs around to the right. Rather than panning over in the direction that the camera is pointing, which would lose the teacher from the shot, the arc lets us see the teacher introducing Winslet's character. The scene is then effectively handed over to Winslet's character, as the camera pushes into a relatively close shot of her.

The camera remains low throughout, which gives Winslet's character far more authority than if it leveled off to her head height. This too helps her to dominate the scene and makes her introduction to the film unforgettable.

Even the most complex moves can be achieved handheld, but you may find a move like this works best if it is precise and strong. A crane and dolly combination would be the best way to achieve this, although you could get a similar effect with a camera stabilizer.

Heavenly Creatures. Directed by Peter Jackson. Miramax Films, 1994.

MOVE WITH CAMERA

Having two or more characters walk and talk is a good way to let a scene unfold at the actors' pace, without the scene being controlled by cutting. This doesn't always work, but if a scene needs to convey a relationship between two people in just a few sentences, it's an effective way to show how they relate. The movement through a location is also a useful way to make a relatively dull conversation a little more visually interesting.

One way to shoot this is to stay directly in front of the actors at all times, and keep the camera at exactly the same distance from them. This can lead to problems when you change direction, however, as the background seems to rush by, and there's a sudden feeling of drama when there shouldn't be. To avoid this, you put in a small move, followed by a larger one, as shown in the frames from *Derailed.*

Begin the shot with the camera directly in front of the actors. They are framed centrally, and the camera moves backward. Then, let the camera move around the corner slowly, as the actors catch up slightly. For a moment the actors will almost be alongside the camera, rather than framed in the middle.

Your camera then continues its move backward along the next corridor, and the actors again become framed in the middle. This small move at the beginning, where you allow the actors to move alongside the camera, prevents too much dramatic motion, and gives the shot far more variety than if you simply stayed in front of them.

When there's no real change of direction, it works well to keep the camera at the same distance, as shown in *The Karate Kid,* and we get to see the actors' relationship from the proximity of their bodies, as well as their expressions.

MOVING STRAIGHT ON

When you push straight in on a subject, this is another strong way to introduce a character, or show that he is important to the upcoming sequence. If you do this too directly, though, the effect can be comical, so there are a few tricks that make this work.

In these frames from *The Adjustment Bureau,* you can see that the camera pushes straight on to Terence Stamp from some distance away. To make this dramatic, rather than comical, the actor on the right (with his back to camera) is moving rapidly toward Stamp. His movement drags the camera along, and makes the whole effect make more sense. If we pushed in this quickly, without that additional movement, there is a strong risk of accidental comedy.

Although that actor provides the motivation for the forward camera movement, the camera eventually catches up and passes him. By this stage, it's acceptable, because the remaining distance is no more than you would get with a normal push in. So when you want to push in rapidly from a long distance, use an actor's movement, off to the side of the frame, to get you most of the way there.

It also helps to have considerable movement in the frame at the beginning, from other actors, and from the wall on the left. By the end of the shot, this movement has been taken away, and Terence Stamp is isolated in the frame. This makes his presence felt far more powerfully than if other actors remained in the shot.

Finally, the entire scene happens at a slightly oblique angle to the set. Rather than heading directly down a corridor at 90 degrees to the opposite wall, the camera crosses the room, and remains at a slight angle to the opposite wall. This softens the move slightly, enabling it to occur quickly without looking over-stylized. Conversely, if you want an extremely stylized look, don't use the oblique angle.

MOVING SIDEWAYS

The best moves remain largely unnoticed by the viewer, but achieve several effects at once. By dollying slowly to the left, while the actors move in a variety of different ways, you can create a complex scene that brings out interpersonal dynamics between the characters.

The frames from *Laurel Canyon* show the camera moving steadily from right to left. The location is ideal for this, as the aisles of the store help to add visual interest because they pass close to the camera, and exaggerate the perspective. They also give the characters motivation to move around. When planning this sort of move make sure there is a reason for the character to move, so that it's easier for the actors, and so that it makes sense on screen. Don't move them around simply to get a good visual.

As the camera moves, the actors change sides within the frame. This is achieved by Christian Bale moving to frame left and turning around as the camera moves to that point. This scene is partly about his avoidance of certain issues, and this setup lets us see that clearly. We see Kate Beckinsale's eyes, gazing almost toward camera, as he moves around shiftily.

Both characters then turn away from the camera, and move back into the shot together in the next aisle. Again, she is following him, giving us the feeling that he is uncomfortable. The camera comes to rest as they do, and she is once again framed on the left, with her expression the dominant one in the scene.

The scene works because of her facial expression and his body language, and it's worth pointing this out to your actors. Some actors want their faces on screen at all times. If your actor tries to achieve that result, it could potentially ruin this sort of scene, Instead, point out the power of body-acting, and let the contrasting acting style work with the camera to get the scene to succeed.

MOVING AT AN ANGLE

By moving at an angle, you can move two characters who are separated by a distance, close together, in a single shot. This scene from *X-Men: The Last Stand* begins with Patrick Stewart and Ian McKellen separated by the car. This gives the impression that they have their differences. By the end of the shot, we are facing both of them, as they stand together. This shows that, for the time being at least, they are going to cooperate.

There are countless ways to shoot two characters coming together from different places, but this move achieves the effect without a cut, and the effect will only be experienced subconsciously by the audience. Patrick Stewart initially dominates the frame, but as the camera moves off at an angle, his size in the frame reduces, as Ian McKellen's apparent size in the frame increases.

It's important to notice that the camera pans around as the camera moves. Initially, it pans to follow the actors, but then it pans hard to the left as the camera arrives in front of the actors, looking back down the street. This has the effect of framing them together, roughly in the center of the screen. It also works as an establishment shot, letting us see where they are without shooting it separately.

To shoot this particular example, you would need the camera to be on a crane and dolly, in order to keep the camera above objects such as the fence. In other locations, the same effect could be achieved with dolly, stabilizer or even handheld.

The shots from *The Road* show a slight push toward the characters, as they struggle across the road with their shopping cart. By having the camera approach the road at an angle, and having the actors move across the road at an angle, we get a feeling of being stuck in a location, rather than moving along it. If the camera was directly alongside the road, or pointing straight down it, this might give the impression that the characters were making good progress. When you want to show a struggle, this angle can achieve that effect.

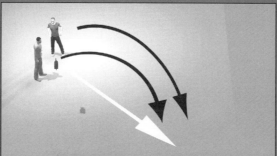

The Road. Directed by John Hillcoat. FilmNation Entertainment, 2009.

X-Men: The Last Stand. Directed by Brett Ratner. Twentieth Century Fox, 2006.

SHORT MOVES

Chase scenes appear in so many movies, but getting them to work well is an art. One thing that is lacking in so many chase scenes is a sense of fear. If you aren't worried about your protagonist, then it's nothing more than a lot of running around.

To create the feeling of fear, it's a good idea to give the impression that the pursuers are catching up with your hero. There are many ways to do this, with the simplest being to show them getting closer. A more interesting way is to use a small camera move to create the sensation of escape.

In these frames from *The Adjustment Bureau,* the camera moves backward slightly during the brief scene. This gives us the slight feeling that we are trying to escape.

Matt Damon rushes toward camera, and out of the frame on the right. As we continue to move backward, the pursuers catch up rapidly. They are moving much faster than him. Their speed, combined with the slow crawl backward, gives us the feeling that we're about to get caught. This leads us to empathize with the character.

During a chase scene it's often tempting to push the camera toward the actors, to exaggerate apparent movement, but be wary of over-using this, because it can make the audience feel too casual about the scene. The occasional slow creep backward can do much to establish the sensation of unpleasant pursuit that's essential if your scene is to have emotional impact.

The Adjustment Bureau. Directed by George Nolfi. Universal Pictures, 2011.

TURNS AND CURVES

Moving the camera in an arc has many effects, depending on whether you're moving with or around your subjects. During the chase scene from *The Karate Kid,* the camera moves with the actor. It stays low, and just ahead of him, as he rushes around a corner.

This sort of rapid, low arc, shot with a short lens, is an excellent way to increase the sense of speed during a chase scene. The short lens makes the walls and objects appear to rush by rapidly. By moving in an arc around the corner, the edge of the wall flashes into frame and obscures the actor for a fraction of a second. This makes it feel as though he's struggling to go as fast as he wants. The other approach to moving in an arc is to start the shot alongside your actors, and then arc around them. As you do, the camera pans to keep them framed. These frames from *Laurel Canyon* show how a dialogue scene is made more visually interesting by arcing around the actors. Only when the camera comes to rest at the end of the shot does the director cut to another shot. In this case it is a jump cut to a shot from the same angle, with a longer lens, but you could cut to just about any other angle, because the arc has so effectively established the space and staging of the actors.

There are many ways to move your camera in an arc. Steadicam or other stabilizers are a common option, but you can also use a combination of dolly and crane. Handheld moves aren't as successful, unless you're following a subject through the scene.

The Karate Kid. Directed by Harald Zwart. Columbia Pictures, 2010.

Laurel Canyon. Directed by Lisa Cholodenko. Sony Pictures Classics, 2003.

CHARACTER MOVES

You can use the depth of a scene to create a moment of tension, without even moving the camera. Depth staging is a way of using the space available to you to tell the story. This can be as simple as making sure you have a foreground, mid-ground and background. Or, as shown here, you can have your characters move through the space where you're shooting, to create an effect.

In these frames from *Blade Runner*, Joe Turkel is not especially close to the camera, and the lens is quite long. This means that when he moves back from the camera, his motion will not be exaggerated. If you wanted the backward motion to be really noticeable, you'd use a short lens. The setup shown here, however, has a different effect. By using a long lens, which throws the background out of focus, and by framing him hard to the left, he almost appears trapped. We can see the space in the room, but it's as though he can't escape the frame.

We then cut to a shot that is out of focus, and Rutger Hauer walks into the frame. This is far more visually interesting than if he'd stayed in focus throughout, and captures the oppressive, nightmarish feeling of the scene. This requires an actor who can hit an exact mark, but it can produce quite a profound effect.

This sort of scene staging gives the viewer the feeling of space, and the feeling of movement through that space, without moving the camera. You can make this even more effective by repeating the move a few moments later. The final frames show how the actor backs off, and this time there is no cut, but we see Rutger Hauer move into the shot. He remains out of focus, a motif that is used through the scene to represent fear.

CROSSING

To make the most of the space you're using, and to indicate where everybody is in the scene, it helps to have the characters cross the scene horizontally. Even if the actors are unclear or out of focus, the movement can help the audience to become oriented within the scene. In some circumstances, this can enhance the story.

The frames from *Love Actually* show one way to set this up. In the wide shot we see the boy sitting in the center of frame, with Liam Neeson crossing the room repeatedly in the background. We cut from this, straight to a close-up on Thomas Sangster's face. As Liam Neeson passes backward and forward in front of the camera, we only see his outline, blurred and dark, but we only need that motion to know where he is.

Having the boy sit centrally within both frames helps to connect the shots. If one was at a slight angle, or if the boy was offset to one side, the motion might not be as clear.

This scene could have been shot with the two characters sitting across from each other at a table, but by having one pace around, there is a sense of nervous tension. The motion is made so obvious, that we feel the unease of the situation. Even though this is a light comedy, the tension is essential, and the staging contributes as much to the scene as the acting.

The second example, from *Black Swan*, shows how you can focus on a background character, and let other people pass in front of the camera. They are not incidental, as such, but we are more interested in what Vincent Cassel's character is observing, and how he feels when observing them, than in observing them ourselves. This is a strong way to emphasize one person's point of view.

If you want to cut to a wider shot, it helps to go really wide. This makes it clear where everybody is in the room, but ensures the other actors are not featured directly, and so our focus remains on the one character and his perception.

MOVE TO FRAME

It's quite common to use objects within a scene to frame another part of the scene. You might shoot through a doorway, using the doorframe to create a frame within the frame. In this example from *Laurel Canyon* you can see how the shot ends this way.

The problem with using a frame within a frame is that the composition can look very stark and stylized. If that's what you're going for, it's no problem, but if you want the frame to draw attention to an image more subtly, it works well when you combine a move with a reveal of the frame.

In this shot, the actors approach the door, and the camera pushes toward them at the same rate. Then as the actors move to the right of the corridor, the camera pans to follow them, and the shot ends with the actors and the door framing the scene behind, drawing our attention through the doorway.

The final framing requires actors on either side of the door. In reality this is probably not how people would stand, leaving a space for the camera to peer through. This is why you need relatively fast motion throughout the shot, to disguise the moment where everybody moves into place. It's a heavily staged final framing, and the quick movement covers the lack of realism.

To achieve this sense of speed, push the camera toward the actors at the same speed they are approaching, then as they move into final positions (some crossing in front of the camera to do so), pan rapidly. The combination of movement covers the move, and makes the effect work.

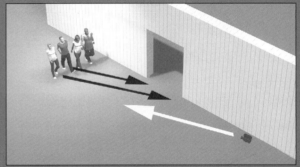

MOVING POINT OF VIEW

When you unexpectedly break away from a character's point of view, it can create interesting reactions in the audience. Depending on the context, these reactions can range from surprise, to a subconscious unease.

The scene from *An Education* begins with a shot of Carey Mulligan walking slowly down the stairs, listening in on the conversation. The shot is long enough to establish that she is moving downward in an arc. When we then cut to a shot moving downward in an arc, we assume we are seeing the scene from her point of view. We are seeing her observation of the characters in the room.

Surprisingly, Mulligan then walks into frame left, and moves into the scene. This is mildly disorienting for the viewer, although most will not consciously notice what's happened. In essence, the character has walked into her own point of view.

In this scene, we initially feel we are sharing the character's secret voyeurism, but when she then joins the scene, we are left feeling as though we are the voyeurs. This sensation makes us uncomfortable, which is precisely what's required for this scene. We aren't sure whom to identify with, who's in the right or wrong, and the camera moves echo this perfectly.

At times of change, or when a character is indecisive, or making a poor decision, this is a perfect device. It works extremely well when there is a sense of sneaking, discovering, or walking slowly, so that we really get time to see the character's body movement, and cut to a camera move that appears to replicate this movement exactly.

MOVE TO REVEAL

When everything remains still, but new things appear in frame due to a camera move, you draw attention to the newly revealed detail. There are many ways to achieve this effect, and even if you don't have access to a dolly or crane you can achieve the effect handheld.

In the first example, from *Harry Potter and the Deathly Hallows: Part 1*, the shot begins with the cottage framed centrally. There is some movement inside, and as the camera pulls back we logically assume that somebody will emerge from the cottage. Instead, the camera moves back until Rupert Grint is in the frame. As it comes to rest, the focus shifts to him.

For the viewer, it feels as though the camera has pulled back in a straight line. In fact, you need to angle the dolly slightly to the left, in order to frame your actor almost centrally. Only by having this angle can you get in front of the actor.

This shot is useful for drawing attention to a character, to show that he is deep in thought, or about to act. It is a dramatic reveal, and suggests the character is separating from the environment or location that opens the scene. Be wary of using this sort of setup arbitrarily. If you simply want to show that the character is outside the cottage, use something less dramatic and surprising.

The second example, from *Bridge to Terabithia*, is less dramatic, with the camera rising up from behind the tractor to reveal the house and truck behind. This is more of a utility shot, a way of establishing a location without resorting to a static shot of the house.

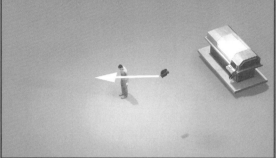

Bridge to Terabithia. Directed by Gábor Csupó. Walt Disney Pictures, 2007.

Harry Potter and the Deathly Hallows: Part 1. Directed by David Yates. Warner Bros. Pictures, 2010.

MOVE WITH REFLECTION

Reflections are sometimes seen as an annoyance on-set, because they show light sources, crew, and other unwanted artifacts. When you learn to use reflections creatively, they become an exciting tool that can be used to create original shots, add visual interest to something that is otherwise uninspiring, or add a layer of symbolism.

The opening frame from *AI: Artificial Intelligence* shows reflections on the windscreen that might not, at first, seem desirable. Many directors would ask the director of photography to hide them, so we get a clear view of the characters. Spielberg leaves them there because they help add depth to the scene. Haley Joel Osment's character is separated from his mother against his will. Having him outside the car as she drives away is the obvious way to show this. A second detail is that the actor places his hand on the glass, showing the barrier between them. But the reflections on the glass enhance this all further, making her appear to be enclosed in a bubble that he can't penetrate.

The next shot is taken directly into the car's wing mirror, which is angled in such a way that as the car drives off, we see Osment recede into the background. This is a highly specific shot that you probably wouldn't want to copy, but it gives you an idea for how reflections on moving objects work.

The final frames show a variation on one of Spielberg's signature shots. He frequently shoots scenes where an actor moves her hand into the frame, holding an object that's relevant to the story. Normally this is achieved with a short lens, to keep everything in focus, and to make the object that is near to camera appear larger than the background. In this example, however, Spielberg is able to use a long lens because we're looking at her reflection. By staging things this way we are able to see her face, and then the perfume bottle, without any cut, simply by pulling focus as she raises her hand. A short lens would create a quirky distortion that wouldn't suit the mood of this scene, so the reflection is an ideal solution for showing two things in quick succession without a cut.

AI: Artificial Intelligence. Directed by Steven Spielberg. Warner Bros. Pictures, 2001. All rights reserved.

REVERSED PUSH

When shooting in two opposing directions, you can push the camera in both directions, to make it clear that a moment of drama is coming. This is a powerful way to show that a fight, chase, or other action scene is about to take place.

In *The Book of Eli,* the camera pushes toward the graveyard at the back of the house. Anytime you push a camera toward something, you make the subject of the shot seem important. To make this even more intense, we then cut to a shot of the four actors observing the graveyard, and we push toward them.

Two static shots could convey the scene, and show that four people are looking at a graveyard, but by pushing in two directions, and cutting between those shots, we sense impending drama and great unease.

The way you move your actors within the frame has a profound effect on this shot. The actors at the back leave the scene, and as they do, Denzel Washington and Mila Kunis move together. As the camera moves closer the angle of view is reduced, so you need to move the actors together to keep them in the frame.

You need to find a way to move your actors that relates to the story. Here, the actors at the back move out of the scene, but then Washington turns to the side, preparing to leave, whispering to Kunis. Ensure that your actors move in a way that makes sense, rather than to suit the shot. The camera is there to serve the story, not the other way around.

VELOCITY DOLLY

When you introduce a character to a film, you can establish her importance by pushing in on her as she moves toward the camera. This has the effect of making her go from relatively small, in terms of the frame, to much larger, and signifies her potential impact on the story. It helps if there are other actors in frame, to give both camera and character somewhere to go.

You can see in these frames from *Inception* that the camera moves toward the male actors, at the same time that Ellen Page moves toward them. It is clear from the beginning of the shot that the actor and the camera are going to end up in the same place.

This works well to establish a space, but then closes in to focus on the dialogue. Rather than showing a wide shot of the room and a series of medium shots, this move enables you to show the room, and then position the camera for the dialogue without a cut. The move is helped by Michael Caine's slight turn away from camera, which pulls us in that direction.

It can be quite difficult to keep focus in a shot like this, where there's camera and actor motion. One solution is to close the camera aperture, but this has the effect of making the background sharper than you may want. That appears to be the case in this shot from *Inception*, where artificial blurring has been added in post.

These frames from *Blade Runner* show a much slower push in. It is essentially the same shot. Daryl Hannah's character is being introduced to the scene, and she moves in slowly, as the camera pushes in slowly, with another character marking the destination of both camera and actor.

Blade Runner. Directed by Ridley Scott. Warner Bros. Pictures, 1982.

Inception. Directed by Christopher Nolan. Warner Bros. Pictures, 2010.

CHAPTER 4

EXPERT FRAMING

LINE CROSS

By using a conventional setup, and then switching from it abruptly, you can create a moment of drama. The first two frames from *Love Actually* show the camera set up in a conventional way, filming each actor in turn, from the same angle and height, staying on one side of the actors.

Even if there were several other angles, the camera would always remain on the same side of the actors, never crossing the imaginary line drawn between them. This is one of the first things you're taught at film school. Draw a line between the actors, and wherever you put the camera, keep it on one side of that line throughout the scene. Most of the time this makes sense, and helps to orient the audience, but a sudden switch has a powerful effect.

At the moment that we hear a noise off camera, we cross the line. The camera is suddenly on the other side of the actors. To make this cut randomly in the middle of the scene would draw attention to the cut, and would feel abrupt, but it comes just as we hear the noise, and is followed by Colin Firth's head turn.

We then immediately cut to a two-shot of the actors. If we'd cut straight to this two-shot from the original setup, it would have felt like a very abrupt cut. The brief shot of the head turn connects everything together. As always, cutting at or around the time that something moves makes the setups flow together seamlessly.

BREAK CUT

One of the most beautiful ways to frame actors is to put the camera alongside them, capturing both faces at the same time. This works while they are looking forward, and even when they turn to each other. It is considered quite a hard angle, however, and presents some problems in editing, so you need to prepare for these.

The first frame from *Blade Runner* shows a perfect example of this hard framing, with a long lens capturing both actors' expressions, even though the focus is sharper on Harrison Ford. Both are staring at the sheet music on the piano, and we cut to this briefly. We don't need to see the sheet music — it's obvious what they are looking at, and from the sounds and how they act. The reason we cut to the sheet music is to create a break between this hard framing and the next shot.

The shot of Sean Young is also quite a hard frame, but not such a tight angle. Even so, cutting around this far would feel almost like a jump cut, so the shot of the sheet music acts as a softener between cuts. When setting up hard angles, be certain to get useful and meaningful cutaways that will enable editing to flow.

The frames from *Bridge to Terabithia* show another approach, with the opening two-shot establishing where the actors are in relation to each other. Once this has been made clear, we cut to a hard framing. Again, both characters are looking outward rather than at each other, and the focus is on Josh Hutcherson.

In the next cut, he looks at AnnaSophia Robb and she turns her head slightly toward him. The angle, once again, is not as hard in this second shot. If it was, then we wouldn't see her face as clearly.

Hard angles, which capture both faces alongside each other, are beautiful, but they can only be used briefly, and need other shots and angles to connect them to the rest of the scene.

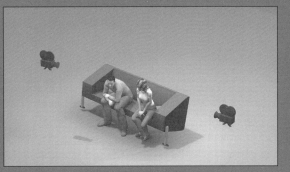

Blade Runner. Directed by Ridley Scott. Warner Bros. Pictures, 1982.

Bridge to Terabithia. Directed by Gábor Csupó. Walt Disney Pictures, 2007.

PAN MOTION

One of the simplest camera moves, the pan, can be used to create elaborate and expressive framing. By combining actor motion with the pan, you create rich shots with minimal effort.

The frames from *The Book of Eli* show the camera panning slowly to follow Denzel Washington, keeping him in roughly the same part of the frame as he moves. Then, as Mila Kunis runs into the frame, the camera pans hard, putting them both on the right of frame. It is as though her movement speeds up the pan.

The shot then continues with them both in this part of the frame. The purpose of this shot is to show her running to catch up and then joining him. As such, it needs to show his pace, then her increased pace, and then the two of them walking at the same pace. If the pan didn't change its pace during the shot, it would not capture these elements. By tying its motion to hers, the meaning of the shot is successfully conveyed.

The frames from *The Karate Kid* show a pan combined with a small dolly motion. The camera dollies from left to right, as it pans from left to right, following the characters as they walk. This shot is used to show the characters returning to a familiar place. If the camera merely panned it would feel as though the actors were rushing past the camera. If you are trying to show extreme pace, that would work, but for a casual walk-in, you need a different effect.

PUSH THROUGH

One of the more interesting ways to frame is by shooting through a group of actors, and then having your main character push through those actors. The opening framing from *Never Let Me Go* shows Nathalie Richard facing a group of schoolgirls. Rather than showing a shot of the girls and then a shot of her, we see her in the distance, appearing tiny in the frame, whereas the girls, although out of focus, are large.

The balance of power is uncertain at this point in the film, but what this opening frame establishes so well is that Richard feels uneasy and overwhelmed by the small group of girls. This framing also effectively shows that the girls are a barrier. She clearly wants to head toward camera, but they are blocking her way.

When she does move forward, the camera creeps back a short distance. This reflects her movement, but gives the feeling that the barrier is still there, as though she is pushing through a barrier, even though the girls move gently aside.

Once Richard is through the barrier, the camera moves back at the same pace as her, so that the girls recede into the background, but we see them turn and watch. This is an elegant move that underlines everybody's unease with the situation.

Don't think of your actors as movable props, but ensure that any time you frame through the actors in this way, there is a good story reason to do so.

Never Let Me Go. Directed by Mark Romanek. Fox Searchlight Pictures, 2010.

REPEAT ANGLE PUSH

By combining a simple move with an unusual angle, you can heighten the atmosphere of a scene. To take this even further, it helps if you use two shots with unusual angles, one after the other.

The opening frame from *The Return of the King* is simple to achieve, but looks stunning. The camera is placed above the actors, pointed at them, and then canted over to the right. When you cant the camera, you lean it over on its side. This makes it look as though Elijah Wood is leaning out toward the left of frame. In itself this is an unusual and effective framing.

We then cut to a reverse shot, looking up at the two actors. The upward angle is much shallower, and we are almost at Elijah Wood's head height, as this move is about his expression. The camera, however, is canted over to the right. By having the canted angle in both shots, they cut together easily.

The camera then pushes in on Wood, and the cant is reduced until the camera is almost level at the end of the push. Both of these shots are easy to achieve – the first with a tripod, the second with a dolly – and yet the final effect feels like a complex crane shot.

If you started the second shot without the cant, the nightmare feeling would be lost, and it would feel more like a moment of realization. By using the cant in both shots, and then reducing it to level, it feels like we're spinning out of control throughout the scene. This gives everything a dreamlike feeling, ideal for a moment of almost overwhelming disorientation.

The Lord of the Rings: The Return of the King. Directed by Peter Jackson. New Line Cinema, 2003. All rights reserved.

TILT REVEAL

Directors are always looking for new and visually exciting ways to reveal information. You may want to introduce a character, establish a space, or show that something is about to happen. When you plan carefully, you can reveal all these details with an actor's movement and a gentle tilt of the camera.

The frames from *Léon: The Professional* show how the shot begins with a low camera, looking up at the actor. He's signaling to somebody behind him, so we suspect somebody is there. Usually, a shot this close would cut to something wide. His unexpected move backward lets us see his fear.

As the camera follows him, tilting down, the rest of the scene is revealed, and we see the other characters waiting with their guns drawn. He joins them, and draws his gun, pointing straight at the camera.

There are many ways this move can be utilized, but it is especially powerful when you want the character's face to remain in shot. You could also do this move in reverse, changing the focus from the wider scene to a close-up of one character.

When you set up a shot, it's always a good idea to think about the strength of your framing at the beginning and end-up shots. Ideally, the framing should be strong throughout. This shot is a good example of a well-framed image through the move.

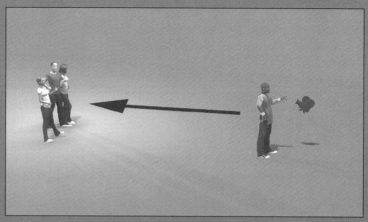

Léon: The Professional. Directed by Luc Besson. Columbia Pictures, 1994. All rights reserved.

ROTATE OUT

This scene from *Blade Runner* is an elegant combination of actor and camera choreography. It includes an arc, and is slightly more difficult to achieve than a dolly or crane shot, but the results are superb.

As you can see, the director has chosen to favor Rutger Hauer for the latter part of the scene, and rather than cutting back to Joe Turkel, he lets the staging remain strong. He may have shot other angles, and more coverage, but as the grace of this shot works to focus on the character's conflict, there is no need for a cut.

The scene begins in what appears to be a standard over-the-shoulder shot, with Hauer's back to us. As he moves around to the left of the other character, the camera arcs around. He turns so that he is facing the camera, and the camera faces him. The other actor remains in place.

From here we are focused on Hauer, but see the other character in the same place, being closely observed. He remains out of focus.

Hauer sits, and Turkel walks across and out of the frame, with Hauer's eyes following him. In the overhead diagram, you can see the arc made by the camera is an almost exact opposite of Hauer's small arc. These opposing arcs make it feel like Turkel is being encircled or trapped. This makes his move out of the frame a brave move, which, in story terms, it is.

When you want an actor to move alongside another, consider arcing around them to frame, and see if you can execute the entire scene without cutting to coverage.

Blade Runner. Directed by Ridley Scott. Warner Bros. Pictures, 1982. All rights reserved.

SILHOUETTE

Silhouettes should not be overused, because they can frustrate the audience by hiding too much, but when used carefully they can have a profound effect. The first thing a silhouette does is make us wonder what a character is thinking. The irony is that the actor cannot convey these thoughts through the face, but has to use body acting. Make sure your actor knows you're shooting a silhouette, so he can adjust accordingly.

The first frames from *The Book of Eli* show this well, with the first making us wonder what Denzel Washington is looking at, what he's deciding. The second, which uses the tunnel as a frame around him, as he stands, makes us wonder where he's going to go next. If these were shot without the silhouette effect, we wouldn't speculate as much.

The two frames from *Bridge to Terabithia* show a more subtle use of this. This scene is from the opening of the film. We don't really know the character yet, so seeing him in silhouette lets us observe that he's an active boy in a rush, but we wonder who he actually is.

The remaining frames, from *There Will Be Blood*, show an extended scene in which Daniel Day-Lewis mumbles to himself before addressing a crowd. He is in silhouette so that we can't be sure of his mood or his intentions, and we wonder whether his thoughts are contradicting his words. He remains in silhouette even as he moves to approach the crowd (they are lit strongly), and this maintains the air of mystery about what his next move will be.

To create a silhouette all you need is a background that is brighter than the subject. This is usually the case when you're using available light, and you need to do nothing more than expose for the background, and let the subject flatten out to black.

DOUBLE PUSH

Every shot needs to reveal character and convey story, but the most skilled filmmakers manage to convey symbolism through their setups. Sometimes this can be a major thematic symbolism, and at other times it can reflect the meaning of a scene or moment.

In this example from *Heavenly Creatures,* the scene is staged in a way that tells that story through the actors' expressions and the camera move itself, rather than what is said. In this scene the characters are ostensibly talking about a serious subject, but the subtext (which screams loudly through the scene) is that they are attracted to each other.

The staging is quite simple, in that we start with two over-the-shoulder shots, and cut between them. Each of these shots, however, is a dolly shot that closes in on the opposing character. During the course of the scene we go from two over-the-shoulder shots to two close-ups.

Although this isolates each character in their own frame, the move does not separate them. Instead it shows how their focus on the other grows, how the other enlarges in their vision, and how they are drawn together.

When you want to show attraction between two people, whether it is spoken or not, close the camera in on both. It can be done rapidly, as in this scene, which has a comical effect, or much more gradually.

MAGNETIC CHARACTERS

Sometimes the staging of your characters tells the story as much as the camera angles themselves. These frames from *Inception* show straightforward shots of the actors, but their positions within the frame, and throughout the scene, affect the impact of the story.

The opening frame shows Ken Watanabe sitting in the plane, looking out at Leonardo DiCaprio. Although DiCaprio is facing toward camera, his body is almost turned away, as though he doesn't want to continue the conversation. Behind him, Joseph Gordon-Levitt has turned his body away. Everything here suggests that Watanabe is leaning into a conversation he wants to continue, while the others are hoping to get away.

DiCaprio then walks back to the plane to continue the conversation, and moves into a close-up. The camera only moves slightly to make sure he is framed well. Behind him, Gordon-Leviit turns to face camera, as though he is being drawn back to the scene.

We then cut back to Watanabe, but this time the shot is closer. In the story, the point that's being made is that this conversation has to take place, and the framing reflects this. The reluctant body language is cancelled out by a rapid move back into frame, and then a series of close-ups. We go quickly from seeing these characters shouting across open space, to seeing them in close quarters.

When you want to show that characters are being drawn to each other, especially reluctantly, you can keep the camera in place, and let body language, acting, and movement to the camera do most of the work. Be prepared to switch one of the shots to a closer angle, to match the close-up from the actor who's in motion.

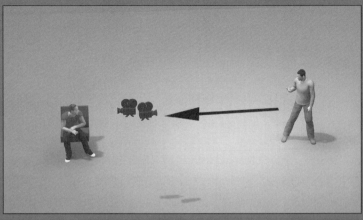

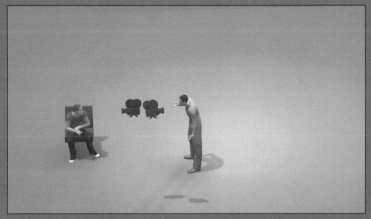

INTIMACY BREAK

Intimacy between characters is essential in most films, but rarely achieved with great success. In *Never Let Me Go,* we see many moments of intimacy that are not overstated, but that remain unmistakable.

These frames show a moment where the characters are uncertain, perhaps even afraid, but they remain connected. For a few moments we doubt this, and that's what makes their renewed intimacy all the more powerful. This is achieved through a sequence of shots, beginning with one where they have their backs turned to each other. They continue to hold hands, despite facing away from each other, which shows the mixture of uncertainty and connection.

The next shot, with a long lens, throws Carey Mulligan out of focus, making her appear more indistinct to Andrew Garfield and for a moment she is isolated from him. But then she returns and faces him directly, reestablishing their intimacy.

Clearly, this is not a setup that you could copy directly, because it is telling a specific story, but the points to note are that you can make enormous use of the frame, to show characters touching and holding on to each other, and that the audience cares about where they look. When they aren't looking at each other, we feel a break in their intimacy.

You can increase a momentary sense of isolation by using a long lens to throw one character out of focus, but then show renewed intimacy by having the actors move into the same place, so both are in focus. Most importantly, make use of eye contact. It's often said that the most intimate shots are those where we look almost directly into a character's eye, but it's also essential that we see characters looking at each other, if we are to sense the bond between them.

Never Let Me Go. Directed by Mark Romanek. Fox Searchlight Pictures, 2010. All rights reserved.

HIGH DRAG

Many times, you want to indicate the apparent power of an individual, and a mix of camera angles can help you to do this. Putting the camera low can make people look powerful, but surprisingly, putting the camera above them can have the same effect, so long as they aren't looking upward. It also helps if they are moving during the shot.

In *Léon: The Professional,* you can see how the camera has been placed above Frank Senger, and is tilted toward him. The camera dollies back as he strides forward. Although the camera is high, this angle makes him appear powerful and in control of his surroundings. The fact that he looks straight ahead, combined with his movement, creates an impression of somebody barging through the scene.

The angle also gives you the opportunity to cut out the faces of any entourage he may have. This enables us to see that he has people with him, following him, but because his face is so dominant in the frame, we assume he is the one with all the power.

The difficulty with a shot such as this is knowing what to cut to afterward. It is so powerful and dynamic that cutting away to a weaker shot would lessen the effect. In this example, the director shifts the focus to a minor character, and we watch him observing the frightening character. The whole gang approaches, almost out of frame, and then slide across screen in front of the minor character. This all has the effect of reemphasizing the power of the character, without losing the movement and flow that was established in the opening shot.

POWER EXCHANGE

Camera placement can have an enormous effect on revealing who holds the balance of power in a scene. Whatever lens you're using, and whatever the framing, the actual camera position can symbolize shifts in power. This is further enhanced by the actor's position in relation to the camera.

In *The Book of Eli,* the scene opens with the camera close to Denzel Washington. We connect with him, and feel that he may have control of the situation despite being outnumbered. When we cut to a reverse of the gang who are watching him, the camera is still close to Washington. It is this placement of the camera close to the actor (whichever way we're looking) that helps us identity with him and feel that he is in control.

The next cut, however, takes us across the street, relatively close to Gary Oldman. As the camera dollies back, Oldman gets closer and closer to the camera. The feeling we get is that whoever's closer to the camera is in control, and here, we've seen that shift directly. Even though the camera is moving away from him, Oldman catches up, taking over the scene.

We then cut to a shot from behind Oldman, but the key point here is that the camera remains close to him. We do not cut back to the original close-up of Washington. Oldman's character has apparently taken the camera away from him and is now in control of the scene and the situation.

You can achieve this effect with cuts, but the move where one character approaches the camera is a clever way to make the transition, so the audience actually feels the character taking over the scene.

The Book of Eli. Directed by the Hughes Brothers. Summit Entertainment, 2010. All rights reserved.

INDECISION

Some of the most memorable scenes involve almost no camera movement, but let the staging of the actor dictate the framing. This scene, from *Love Actually,* shows a moment of agonizing indecision for Andrew Lincoln's character, and remains one of the most memorable shots, despite there being almost no camera move.

He enters at frame right, and moves toward the camera, which tilts up and centers him. This gives us an effective medium close-up, but then, surprisingly, he heads away from the camera, which tilts down to follow him. He is, however, kept in the center of the frame.

For the next few moments he moves backward and forward, uncertain whether to stay or go, and his indecision is reflected by the framing, which keeps him locked in the center of the frame. This is why it was important to show him entering the scene hard on the right of frame. At that point he was rushing out with certainty, but the moment indecision strikes, the camera traps him in the middle of the frame. It is only when he finally makes a decision that the camera stays exactly where it is, and he walks out of the frame, breaking free from his situation.

When a character is being indecisive, a central framing can help to show his feeling of indecision. By introducing a slight tilt you can give the actor great freedom to move toward and away from the camera, which is important in scenes that rely on body acting as much as facial expressions.

ISOLATING PUSH

There are moments in a film where you want to show intimacy between characters, which excludes a third party. Although the actors' performances are essential for this to work, you can use two camera moves to enrich the feeling.

In *Heavenly Creatures,* the opening frame shows the two girls, with the camera placed behind Sarah Peirse. This is like an over-the-shoulder shot, except it is shot from the low angle. The reverse shows all three people, but from here all appears to be well, everybody is smiling, and all three people take up roughly the same amount of frame.

Both cameras then push in. The camera that's on the mother moves close to her, staying at the same low level, and looking up. The camera that's pointed at the girls stays slow, and pushes in until they fill the frame.

Having the girls on one level and the mother on another immediately works to create a feeling that the girls are bonding, and that she is separated from them. The final frames isolate the characters from each other, but what's so beautiful about this shot is that we see the isolation happen during the dolly moves.

As the camera pushes in on the mother, the girls drift out of her frame. As the camera pushes in on the girls, the mother drifts out of their frame. We feel the mother being left alone, and we sense the desperate friendship between the girls.

This combination of moves can be used when everybody's on the same level, but having people at different levels really increases the effect, so long as it can be justified in terms of story.

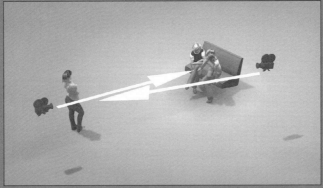

Heavenly Creatures. Directed by Peter Jackson. Miramax Films, 1994. All rights reserved.

GROUP BREAK

When you've set up a good group conversation, you can create a substantial impact without any camera moves, by rearranging the position of the actors on-set.

It is challenging to stage a conversation between three people, because you require a lot of setups to get everybody's face in shot, and you can end up cutting rapidly between all these setups. One good solution is shown in this scene from *Never Let Me Go.*

Although there are three people, and all are involved in the conversation, the main focus is the conversation between the two women. Look at the opening frame, and imagine that the man isn't there. It looks almost like a conventional over-the-shoulder shot. The next two shots are conventional over-the-shoulder shots, but because of that opening group shot, it feels more complex than that.

This scene really takes off, and becomes beautifully dramatic, when the characters move to their next positions. At a critical point in the script, everybody moves. Carey Mulligan walks away from camera, passing Keira Knightly, who moves back in to the place where Mulligan was standing. At the same time, Andrew Garfield moves away from them. You can see these moves in the overhead diagram, and although they are simple, the effect on screen is astonishing, because in a moment, everybody is in their own frame.

With a few simple steps, a group that was so tightly knit has been broken apart. Having Mulligan pass Knightly makes this look more naturalistic than if everybody simply backed away from the group.

If you're shooting a scene where disagreement is increasing, consider starting with a tightly knit group, and then move them out in their own frames. This works well when the conversation continues, but could work even if the characters all continued to walk away from each other.

Never Let Me Go. Directed by Mark Romanek. Fox Searchlight Pictures, 2010. All rights reserved.

CHAPTER 6

PRODUCTION DESIGN AND LOCATION

ANTI-ESTABLISHMENT SHOTS

Traditional establishment shots, where you show a location from a distance before seeing a scene take place, can become tiresome. Audiences used to expect many establishment shots, to break up scenes, and that remains the case in television, although to a lesser extent. Directors have learned to be more creative, so that even when some sort of establishment shot is required, it is handled with grace and ingenuity.

Although you can show a wide shot of your location, and then cut to the main scene, there are countless opportunities to introduce the scene in a more interesting way, revealing story at the same time.

The shot from *The Road* begins with a framing that could be said to be a classic establishment shot, but the camera is already in motion. Slowly, it dollies forward and to the right. This is a slow, gentle move that reveals more of the location, but also an important story point: The shopping cart has been left alone. If you can use an establishment shot to reveal story in this way, the audience won't ever feel they've watched an establishment shot.

In *The Book of Eli,* we start with a shot of the sky. The camera is low, which means that when Denzel Washington walks past the camera it has to tilt down to follow him. In tilting down, the location is revealed. The establishment of the location seems incidental, even though it is the main purpose of this shot.

The Road. Directed by John Hillcoat. FilmNation Entertainment, 2009.

The Book of Eli. Directed by the Hughes Brothers. Summit Entertainment, 2010.

DIRTY FRAME

To make your shots interesting, consider using a "dirty frame." Let props, people, walls, and other intrusions come into the frame, between the camera and the subject. This adds a visual richness that sets scenes apart from the ordinary.

It's easier to dirty the frame when using a long lens, as the foreground objects get thrown out of focus more easily. In an ideal situation, the framing also establishes aspects of story or details about the location.

In these frames from *Blade Runner,* the machine on the table is the most obvious intrusion, but the table itself has also been included in the frame. This means that only the character is in focus. We concentrate on him, but are aware of his surroundings. Also, by seeing the machine on the table, we are less surprised when it's featured a few seconds later.

The same machine dirties the next frame, appearing right in the center of the frame. When you place an intrusion so centrally, you may find that you need to dirty all the frames in a scene, otherwise it will stand out too much.

Imagine these scenes without the dirty frames. We'd see two people sitting at a desk, and nothing more. Instead, we see the machine that will soon be part of the story, and a lush framing.

The third frame shows a candelabrum used to dirty the frame to the extent that it almost obliterates the subject, William Sanderson. This is an ideal way to show somebody in hiding, or even trapped.

The next two frames, of Ellen Page in *Hard Candy,* show a more subtle use of the technique. The blurred objects, and the other actor's hand, appear in both shots, which makes her feel connected to him. This reflects the intense look we see in her eyes, and there can be no doubt that she's concentrating on the character she's looking at.

The final frames, also from *Hard Candy,* show an even subtler dirty frame. As the camera follows the actor to the door, we see parts of the gate and other plants. This reinforces the idea that this house is locked away from the rest of the world, which is an important story point.

Blade Runner. Directed by Ridley Scott. Warner Bros. Pictures, 1982.

Hard Candy. Directed by David Slade. Lionsgate, 2005.

ENRICH THE FOREGROUND

By using background actors to frame your subjects, you can create a sense of a crowded, active room. When you've established a crowd, breaking away from it can show a character's loneliness or longing.

Even with a limited number of background actors, you can create the sense of a crowd, with careful framing. The first shot from *The Fighter* shows Mark Wahlberg, quite small in the frame. A long lens is used, so that the background actors who dominate the foreground are out of focus. By placing them relatively close to the camera, and having him far away, the room seems crowded, even though there are no more than two or three extra people in the shot.

The technique is repeated for a slightly closer view of Amy Adams. Again, two or three people frame her. Rather than just having them on either side, the director has cleverly given the actors a motivation to raise their arms, so they frame her completely.

Now that the crowd has been established, we cut to a closer shot of Wahlberg, and nobody else is in the frame. This lets us watch his expression and sense his longing. If other people remained in this shot, we wouldn't feel the emotion as clearly as when he's placed alone in the frame.

The final cut, back to Adams, is even closer on her, but other people remain in the shot with her. This further stresses that she is out of reach, hidden away by barriers that could be social, personal, or practical.

These are extremely simple setups, in technical terms, but it's the thought behind them that makes this work. When setting up scenes in crowded rooms, consider what your characters are feeling, and know when it's right to see them alone. Even if you can't frame them completely on their own, you can probably frame them so no other faces are visible, which would have a similar effect.

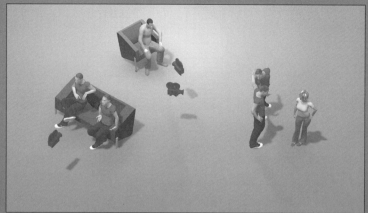

The Fighter. Directed by David O. Russell. Paramount Pictures, 2010. All rights reserved.

FAKE WALL

When working in studios, it is common to have "wild walls" that can be wheeled out of the way to enable you to put the camera exactly where you want it to be. When working on location, you don't have that luxury, so compromises have to be made.

Unfortunately, many directors working on location let the restrictions of the location dictate the shots. If they can't move the wall out of the way, they don't bother to shoot from that direction. More creative directors use a little imagination, and simply pretend there's a wall there when there isn't.

The first frame from *Heavenly Creatures* shows the teacher apparently writing on the board. There may well be a piece of board held up for her to write on (to make her arm movements seem realistic), but she is not standing anywhere near that wall. She has been positioned a few feet into the classroom, with the camera quite close to her face. In the next shot, she turns away from the wall, and the audience never suspects that anything has been faked.

In *Hard Candy,* the opening clearly establishes the wall and the pictures that they are going to observe. This means that when we cut to their close-ups, we don't doubt that they are standing right next to that wall, looking at the pictures. In reality, they will be a good few feet into the room, to make space for the camera.

When shooting this sort of setup, it's vital that you place something alongside the camera for the actors to focus on. If they focus on the actual wall behind the camera, it will make a difference to the focus of their eyes, and this shows up in camera. The illusion will be destroyed. When you give them something to focus on, at the correct distance, they will be able to acquire the right level of focus in their eyes.

Heavenly Creatures. Directed by Peter Jackson. Miramax Films, 1994.

Hard Candy. Directed by David Slade. Lionsgate, 2006.

FRAMING THROUGH

There are many opportunities on-set to film through objects, vehicles, windows, and other structures that obscure the view. This is similar to using a "dirty frame," but here the object is not to enrich the foreground with an out-of-focus object, but to reframe the action. Many effects can be achieved with this reframing.

In the first frame from *AI: Artificial Intelligence,* the car is symbolic of the impending separation; the mother is about to leave her son by driving away in that car. By framing the two of them through the car, we sense that she is trying to get back to it, and he is trying to keep her away.

In *The Book of Eli,* the character is also framed through the ruined structure of a car. It's more interesting for us to begin the shot in the car, and have him approach the camera, than to shoot him from outside the car, and then cut to a shot of him exploring the inside. This is a practical way to achieve the shot without a cut, but also far more visually interesting due to the opportunities to use silhouettes for framing.

The setup from *Inception* uses the windows to create fear. By exposing the shot so that the outside appears correctly lit, the inside of the room seems dark. This focuses our attention on the character running past the windows. Even though he's moving rapidly, it's easy to see that he has a gun. Because the camera is kept stationary as he runs past these window frames, we feel as though we're not moving, which creates the feeling that he's catching up. This is an excellent device to use during chase scenes, when you want the audience to feel as though the pursuer is gaining an advantage.

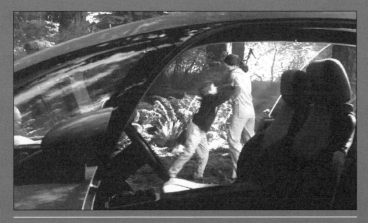

AI: Artificial Intelligence. Directed by Steven Spielberg. Warner Bros. Pictures, 2001.

The Book of Eli. Directed by the Hughes Brothers. Summit Entertainment, 2010.

Inception. Directed by Christopher Nolan. Warner Bros. Pictures, 2010.

FRAMING FOCUS

Window frames offer you many opportunities for creative shots. It's best to work with window frames that contain small panes of glass, otherwise you're shooting through pure glass, and there isn't enough frame to make the effect work.

The shot from *Schindler's List* opens with the actor moving to frame right, coming from behind the windows, and then arcing around to the left. This effectively establishes that the windows are there, and that the character is coming from the room behind them. This is vital to orient the viewer. Without this opening, what follows may feel like the actors are outside the building, staring in.

As he moves further to the left, and peers through the window, we pull focus to Liam Neeson in the distance. The framing effect is further enhanced by the other actors on the left of the screen. Their position is not overly realistic, because if they wanted to peer through, they would move into position to do so, but this moment is so brief that the arrangement still works.

We cut quickly to a shot from roughly the same position, with a longer lens. This prevents us from identifying with the observing characters too strongly. This is not their story, and they have served their purpose by making us want to observe Neeson voyeuristically. We now do that.

The lighting on the window frame changes at the cut. This may be deliberate, because the brightly lit frame may have overwhelmed the shot. Although the change in lighting is not realistic either, it is not noticeable when watching the film. You can get away with such continuity problems if the storytelling of your camera moves is strong enough.

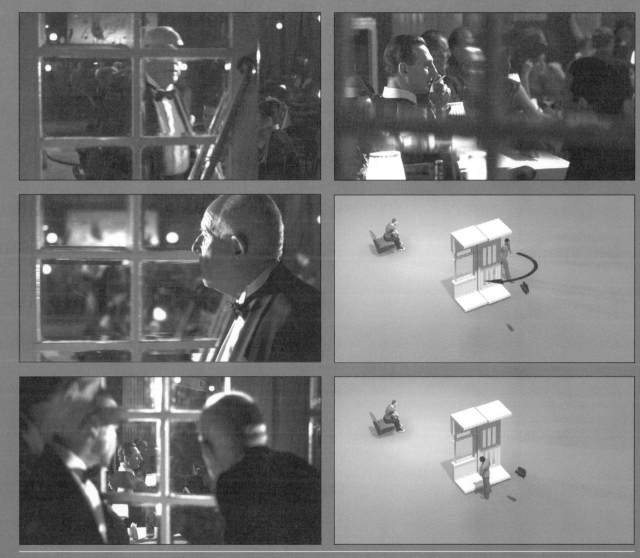

Schindler's List. Directed by Steven Spielberg. Universal Pictures, 1993. All rights reserved.

PERSONAL REVEAL

One character's movement can be used to introduce us to a scene, and then hand over the scene to a second character. In this scene from *Cast Away,* the boy enters the room and leads the camera all the way over to Tom Hanks.

The camera's motion is quite extreme, but doesn't feel overdone, because we are following the boy. Initially, this is a pan, as the boy moves from frame right to the center of the screen. The camera moves to keep up with him, arcing around the room as he does.

His focus shifts to Tom Hanks, on top of the ladder, and the camera is panned so the boy moves to the left of frame. Focus now shifts to Hanks, even though he remains a good distance away.

The camera is still moving in a continuous arc, but now it is heading for Hanks. He comes down the ladder and meets the camera, where it comes to rest.

A shot like this takes a lot of setting up and rehearsal, but in a few short seconds we have seen important story elements (the FedEx delivery arriving), we've established the space, and we've been given a dramatic introduction to the lead character.

To get a shot like this to work, plan the motion of the shot first. Know where you want it to start, and where you want it to end, and then find a way to choreograph the actor's movement to draw the camera through the scene, handing the motion over to the second actor.

Scenes like this are not simple to design or execute, but the time taken on setting them up can easily compensate for the time it would take to shoot lots of coverage.

Cast Away. Directed by Robert Zemeckis. 20th Century Fox (USA/Canada) DreamWorks (International), 2000. All rights reserved.

REFLECTION ESTABLISHMENT

Reflections are a powerful tool for filmmakers, because they enable you to see in two directions. They can be employed to open scenes in ways that are more creative than a wide shot, or a basic close-up.

The first frames from *AI: Artificial Intelligence* show an alternative to opening with a wide shot and then going in for a close-up. Instead, we see Frances O'Connor in the reflection, and then the dinner enters the shot, obscuring her face. From here, we cut to the wide and get an overview of the scene.

It doesn't matter that she's upside down in the opening of the shot, because all we need to see is that she's the one putting the dinner down. Using the reflection enables us to see this with two shots, rather than showing a wide, then the dinner, and then a close-up of her face. There is nothing inherently wrong with shooting lots of coverage and letting the editor decide the rhythm of the scene, but shots like this are beautiful and economical, achieving many of the results you want without a single camera move or cut.

The second example illustrates reflections being used to show two things at once. O'Connor is reflected in the metal lid of the coffee jar. This establishes that she's making coffee, and also shows her in a slightly distorted way, which reflects that way that Haley Joel Osment's character is viewing her.

When we cut to him, his face is reflected in the table, just below the eyeline. This is an inventive way of showing that he's experiencing some degree of conflict. We get a greater understanding of his thoughts than if we saw his whole face.

By starting with the obscure close-up reflections, we focus on the characters, wonder what they're thinking, and anticipate the location and situation being revealed.

AI: Artificial Intelligence. Directed by Steven Spielberg. Warner Bros. Pictures, 2001.

REVERSE REFLECTION

When you begin working with reflections you quickly see the enormous potential of this device, as well as the complications. It can be difficult to light for shots with lots of reflections, and you have to remain constantly aware of getting cameras, cables, and crew in the shot. Despite these challenges, you can use reflections, and more specifically, mirrors, to create extremely rich shots.

The first frame from *Black Swan* shows an elaborate setup that uses one main mirror in the background, which enables us to see the character's form, and her face, in the same shot. The general clutter, so important for the realism of this scene, is also featured in duplicate, adding to the sense of disarray. A second mirror, on the right, gives us an additional view of the character's back. To get this would, in fact, take another off-screen mirror — we're seeing a reflection of a reflection, which is why it appears the right way around. As well as making the shot interesting, this helps reflect the double personalities and illusions that are present in the film.

The second frame uses the same technique to show Natalie Portman's face in two different parts of the frame. The other character, in the background, also appears twice. Be prepared to do a lot of experimenting with your mirrors, especially the off-screen mirror, to get the result you want.

A side benefit of using mirrors is that any space looks larger and yet more crowded when there are mirrors in the shot, because you're looking in two directions at once. This means your crew will all be bunched up in one corner, but makes for extremely rich shots.

A simpler use of mirrors is shown in *The Road,* where we get to see both characters' expressions through the reflections. There is no need to put both characters in the frame. Having Viggo Mortensen in the middle of the shot makes it clear where the boy is standing, especially when Mortensen turns his head to look at him. A shot like this is useful when you want to show characters assessing themselves but still communicating with each other. By using two mirrors, each actor's face is given a mini-frame. A large mirror would reflect the whole room, rather then picking out their faces for us to concentrate on.

Black Swan. Directed by Darren Aronofsky. Fox Searchlight Pictures, 2010.

The Road. Directed by John Hillcoat. FilmNation Entertainment, 2009.

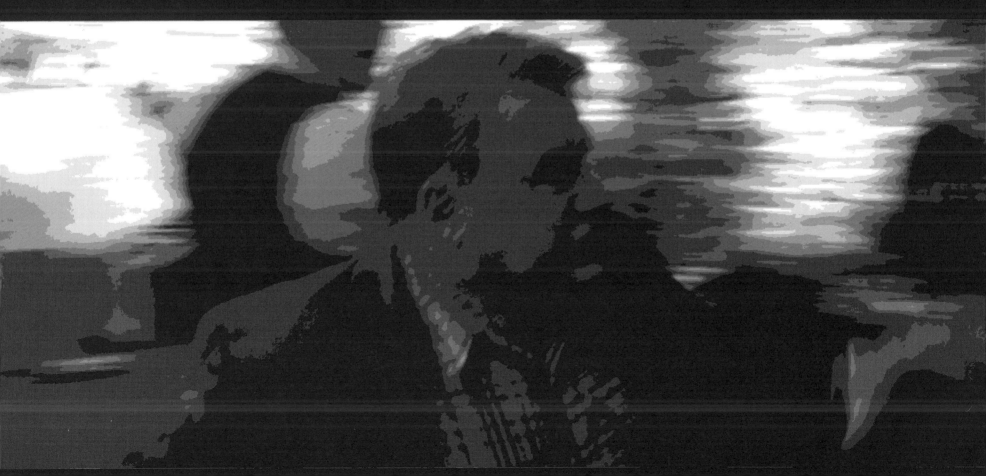

ACTION SHIFT

Action sequences and chase scenes need a lot of movement, and one of the best ways to get this sense of frantic action is to combine two different types of motion. When put together in one shot you get a more compelling sense of motion than if you cut quickly between shots. Fast cutting is a dissatisfying solution to creating a sense of pace, and it's more impressive if you can create the effect in camera.

In this shot from *The Adjustment Bureau,* you can see that the camera is placed almost in Matt Damon's way, and as he rushes past, the camera pans with him. This creates a good sense of pace, because he closes up rapidly and shoots past at great speed.

The camera stops panning, letting Damon run out of the shot. Immediately, his pursuers appear in the shot. They do not follow from behind, as we'd been expecting, but arc from the left, from either side of the stairs that Damon has just climbed.

The sudden appearance of the pursuers is a surprise, because we're waiting for the distant pursuer to catch up. This alone increases the pace of the scene. Also, the fact that they appear just as he's moving out of shot means the viewer gets two sets of rapid motion in the same shot.

When creating action sequences, see if you can find ways to combine shots and motions, bring characters in unexpectedly. You can move the camera in part of the shot, then leave it steady, as shown here, or experiment with moving the camera throughout, or even work with a completely stationary camera. So long as you combine motion from different directions, you should achieve a similar effect.

MISDIRECTED MOTION

Action doesn't always mean fast motion in every frame. Surprise is as important as movement. Creating a moment of surprise is difficult, because audiences tend to sense that you're misdirecting them when everything goes still and quiet.

One solution is to create a moment that feels as though the film is pausing for a moment, but add a camera move. If your shot is too static, the audience suspects a surprise is coming.

This scene from *Blade Runner* shows Harrison Ford making a big deal out of yawning and relaxing in the elevator. His performance, combined with the slow arc around him, convinces us that the action's over for the moment.

Then, he turns suddenly, arcing in the same direction that the camera just moved, bringing his gun right up to the lens. The speed of the move adds to its impact, as does the proximity of the gun to the lens. Also, we have no idea what he's reacting to, because it's behind us, which further adds to the feeling of fear.

Having the camera low is not essential for this type of shot, but works well here because it means the lens is close to arm-level, and thus the gun, when he makes his move. The same shot could be achieved at head height, or even from above, if you aren't so concerned about framing a gun. Instead, you could have him turn, and then have somebody else rush into the shot, or have him rush out. There are thousands of alternatives, so long as you combine a slow dreamy move with a sudden countermove.

Blade Runner. Directed by Ridley Scott. Warner Bros. Pictures, 1982. All rights reserved.

RETURN TO SUBJECT

When you have one character moving fast in a scene, it can be useful to have another moving slowly. The slow-moving character can act as a focus for the scene, so that the camera is drawn back there after the action has passed. This is especially useful when a chase scene or action sequence is coming to an end.

In *The Fighter* we begin the shot with Mark Wahlberg walking toward camera. He's approaching Christian Bale, who's off screen, behind the camera. In the background, Jack McGee rushes up. Although we begin the shot panning slowly with Wahlberg, we pick up McGee as he passes, and pan rapidly with him. His momentum takes him straight into a fight with Bale, and in an instant the two men drop to the ground.

As they fall out of the frame, the camera returns to Wahlberg. It is this return to the slow-walking Wahlberg that indicates the chase is over. If we followed the other two down to the floor, we'd be expecting a brawl.

This particular scene relies on story elements that may not be present in your film, but the move can still work so long as you have one slow-moving character and another who rushes past. The slow move may be motivated by fear, injury, or something else altogether. When creating your shots, take the mechanics of these scenes and apply them to your own, so you ensure they reflect your own story elements.

An alternative ending to this shot would be for the camera to follow McKee and Bale, who begin fighting while standing, and then have Wahlberg walk slowly into the frame to break them up. It is the contrast between different paces of motion that makes this shot interesting.

The Fighter. Directed by David O. Russell. Paramount Pictures (US), 2010. All rights reserved.

PAUSED PUSH

In many modern action scenes, everything moves at once, so there's just a jumble of motion and it's difficult to see what's going on. A more elegant approach to action requires more skilled fight choreography, but enables you to shoot in a more refined way. The result is that we actually get to see the fighting, rather than just get an impression of it through fast cutting.

This does mean, of course, that you're required to get a good stunt coordinator to prepare the scene realistically. If you have that luxury, then this move is an excellent way to showcase the work that's been done. Fortunately, your fight can be quite relaxed and this particular setup will make it look far more energetic.

In these frames from *The Phantom Menace* you can see that an extremely short lens is being used, because the vertical lines are quite distorted. A lens this short makes anything that moves away from it appear to rush by at great speed. This means that when Ray Park backs into the shot, he does so with surprising speed.

Liam Neeson follows him into the shot, pushing him backward. Again, the relatively sedate fight is made to look far more dramatic because of the way the lens distorts space. The lightsabers appear to be moving faster than they are, and everybody appears to be rushing back much faster than they are.

The camera remains stationary until Ewan McGregor rushes in from the side, and then it begins a slow push in. Although we are moving forward, the characters continue to move away from the camera. Without the push, the scene would feel quite static, but with too much motion we'd catch up to the actors.

PUSH AGAINST FLOW

In any action sequence, a sense of frustration can develop the underlying feeling of tension. This is especially important when there's a lot of movement going on in the buildup to a fight. In this scene from *Léon: The Professional,* everybody is running around with their guns, getting ready for a gunfight, and although there's no action as such, there is excitement and tension. This is an ideal time to put in a shot that feels slightly frustrating.

In these frames you can see that the camera pushes forward at the same time that the actors run through the doorway. One character remains in place, and we can tell that we are heading toward him, but our progress feels impeded by the actors rushing through, and it also feels like we are getting in their way.

This shot is over in a couple of seconds, so this is not a lingering frustration, but a subtle and subconscious feeling that things are difficult. This is enhanced at the end by having the actor we've been approaching turn his back to the camera. We've pushed all the way through, only for him to turn away. This small detail adds to the feeling that all is not going according to plan.

In the overhead diagrams you can see something that isn't readily apparent from watching the film, unless studied closely: The actors run forward, then to frame left. This means they can run almost directly at the camera to begin with, but then peel off to their right. Having them run straight off to the right would reduce the impact of their forward rush.

MOTION CIRCLE

Whether you're shooting a fight or a training scene, such as this one from *The Karate Kid,* circling around your characters is a commonly used shot. To make it into something great, a few small adjustments can increase its impact.

The overhead diagram shows the most basic way to move the camera. You arc around the characters, keeping the camera quite low, while they remain in roughly the same place. Throughout the shot, you keep the actors as close to the center of the frame as possible.

This works well enough, but to make it more interesting, you can increase the sense of motion by altering your distance from the actors. The camera keeps the same distance for a while, but by the third frame it has moved away by a few feet. This creates a pulsing sensation within the shot that makes it feel like everything is happening fast.

You can also see in the same frame that the camera goes behind a pillar. Having something pass in front of the camera does a lot to make this move feel fast. When the move feels fast, so does the action. Even if your actors are fighting quite slowly, this will make their move appear faster.

Once the camera is alongside the actors it begins to move back in toward them, further increasing the sense of speed. You will need to use a camera stabilizer for this sort of shot, and a competent operator, to keep the framing stable, while altering distance and circling around.

The Karate Kid. Directed by Harald Zwart. Columbia Pictures, 2010. All rights reserved.

CONVEYING SPEED

Chase scenes are widely used, but to get them to work you need a good understanding of motion. When you choose your angles carefully, you don't need to cut rapidly to convey speed. By shooting angles that are near opposites, one quick cut can create more of a sense of speed than lots of fast cuts.

In these frames from *The Adjustment Bureau,* the speed is conveyed by having Matt Damon run in the exact center of frame. He stays at the same distance from the camera, and remains framed in the exact middle of the shot, as the street closes around him. He doesn't move within the frame, but the world moves around him, and this is what creates the sensation of speed.

We then cut to a shot from directly behind him. Although the camera is now rushing in the opposite direction, we feel Damon's momentum down the street, because this shot is a near exact replica of the first.

The angles are not exact, however, and in the second shot the camera is lower. A low camera will always make a shot like this appear faster, because the ground appears closer and we sense it rushing by. With this being the case, it makes sense for the second shot to have a lower camera, as the chase speeds up. If your actor was coming to a halt, then you might want a higher camera. You could even have the camera crane away from the ground during the second shot, to reduce the sense of motion.

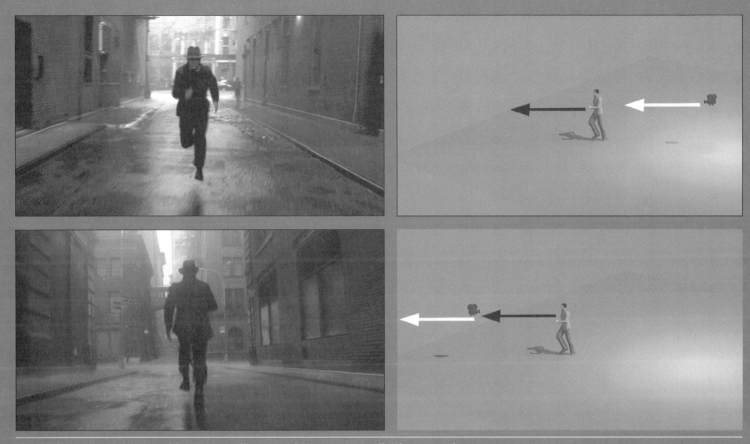

TURN CUT

By combining simple blocking with a quick cut, you can produce the feeling that the action is about to take off. When you're about to have a character rush off to a fight, attempt to escape, or do something else dramatic, this is a good way to show that the decision has been taken and it's time for action.

In these frames from *The Phantom Menace,* Ray Park is looking at a floating droid. Whether you use a droid or another actor, the principle remains exactly the same. At the moment of decision, he turns to his left, while remaining in the same position. At exactly the same time, the droid circles around to his left.

Imagine how different this would be if Ray Park turned to his right. Somehow, that would feel as though he was merely turning around. But because the droid goes to one side, and he turns the opposite way, we get a feeling of things unfolding.

Halfway through this move, we cut to a camera on the opposite side, which immediately dollies backward as Ray Park walks forward. By cutting into this shot, just as the dolly begins, we get the sensation that everything is in motion.

The first shot shows decision, and the second shows action being taken. If you're working with actors (rather than CGI droids), you'll need to make sure the timing is identical for each direction, to ensure that the second frame captures both characters. If you can, shoot with two cameras so that the cuts are guaranteed to match.

CHAPTER 8

SHOOTING PERFORMANCE

OPENING THE SCENE

Scenes with lots of characters can be challenging to handle. This is even truer when the scene involves the introduction of one group of characters to another. In this scene from *Laurel Canyon,* the couple enter and meet a roomful of people. It would be tempting to cover this from ten or more angles, but this scene is achieved with three simple setups.

By limiting the number of setups, you do the actors a favor. If they know the scene is being covered with two shots, they can put everything into those two shots. When you're shooting ten setups, the actors may hold back to reserve their energy. If you can shoot a potentially complex scene with a small handful of setups, then you'll get far better performances. Your choices in editing may be more limited, but this is often a worthwhile gamble.

The scene opens with a low shot of the couple walking in. The whole scene is shot from this angle, but we only cut back to it briefly. This is because the reverse is choreographed to show all the characters' faces and reactions.

The reverse begins with Frances McDormand in the center of the screen. There is more light on her than any of the other actors, and she is the focus of the shot. As the couple move into place, the camera dollies to the right. This enables us to see McDormand rise to join them, briefly placing herself in the middle of frame. During this section, the couple turn to look at her so we see their faces.

As the camera continues its move to the right, McDormand moves to the left, and we pan with her. This small movement is almost like a new shot, and sets us up to cut to a third setup, which is a basic over-the-shoulder of the couple. With one small camera move, and two other simple setups, you get a beautifully choreographed scene. Each time the scene pauses, it looks like a complete, perfectly composed shot.

As always, when constructing this sort of master shot, make sure that composition is good through the scene, rather than just at the beginning and end.

Laurel Canyon. Directed by Lisa Cholodenko. Sony Pictures Classics, 2003. All rights reserved.

BODY ACTING

The best actors know that the emotions you convey with your body are as important as those you convey with your face and voice. The best directors also know this, and ensure that they give actors the opportunity to show how much they can communicate from their posture.

This sequence from *Léon: The Professional* shows how you can create a scene that enables the actors to perform with gestures and body acting, while also conveying an imbalance of intimacy between them.

The scene is effectively from Natalie Portman's point of view, and shows her trying to get the attention of Jean Reno. By beginning the scene on her level, with Reno walking past out of focus, we identify with her as the point-of-view character.

The next frame is a beautiful variation on over-the-shoulder, but we look over the top of her head, and Reno is in the exact middle of the frame. This angle and framing make us very aware of his posture, and he can communicate the character's discomfort with almost no dialogue.

The reverse is not shot from his head height, but from about half his height — otherwise it would feel as though we were looking down on her, and this would make it impossible to see the scene from her point of view. In this frame and the next we get to see her displeasure, partly through her expression, but also through her slouch. A lesser director might be tempted to go for a close-up, but what happens in the body is more important in a scene where characters are struggling to communicate and connect.

The final frame is again a variation on the over-the-shoulder shot, with her blurred head dominating the frame, and Reno quite tiny in the distance. Although he is distant from the camera, we can see all the gestures made through his body acting.

When shooting scenes where strangers meet, or where there is uncertainty between two people, find creative ways to show the gestures they make with their bodies, and be certain to let your actors know you are shooting this way.

CORE CLOSE-UPS

You could say there is no more basic shot than the close-up. Most scenes, in film and television, feature close-ups, so that we can see the actors' faces and hear what they are saying. There is no doubt that you'll use plenty of close-ups in your career, but the trick is to make them interesting while contributing to the story.

In any scene, the instinct of both actors is to face each other and deliver lines. It's how most scenes are played out, and it's the comfort zone we resort to. For the director, it's the easiest thing in the world to point the camera at each of the actors, capture the performance, and move on. If you want to go beyond this, every time you shoot dialogue consider how you could vary this cliché.

The simplest way to generate ideas is to change the actors' body angles, in relation to each other, and in relation to the camera. The first frame from *The Road* could easily have been a standard close-up, shot over the shoulder. Instead, we see Charlize Theron facing neither the camera nor the other character. Although she is on the right of frame, by positioning her at this angle her profile is in the center of frame. This is much more dramatic than if she was looking straight at the other character.

The framing of Viggo Mortensen is more conventional, because if you string together five original framings, you might end up with a scene that's difficult for the viewer to follow. The next frame, with Theron in an embrace, is a more inventive way of showing her face in close-up than moving the camera closer.

The second set of frames shows an approach where both actors' faces appear in medium close-up, in the same frame. When shooting this sort of scene, the challenge is whether to shoot in profile (as they look at each other) or have them face camera (which means that they are facing away). If the story justifies it, the approach shown here is the best; you get the actors to show profile and face camera.

The key to all these close-ups is the position of the actors, rather than the camera. When shooting close-ups or dialogue, you might want to position your actor before you even think about where to put the camera.

EXTREME CLOSE-UPS

Extreme close-ups are often considered a stylistic choice, rather than a way to shoot performance, but so long as you let the actors know that's what you're shooting, you can get great results from these shots.

You need to use an extremely long lens, close enough to the actor that you focus on only the mouth, hands, eyes, or other feature. When using a lens this long, you can widen the aperture so that only one part of the image is in focus. In the first frame from *Léon: The Professional,* the focus is on the tip of the cigarette. When shooting extreme close-ups, actors will often switch to a subtle acting technique, but let them know if they are going to be out of focus, as they will need to raise the performance slightly.

The second frame, on the eyes, is the sort of shot that a good actor will respond to well. You are not simply getting a shot of the eye. You are shooting the whole scene in extreme close-up, to capture the reactions and emotions that are shown in that one eye.

The third frame shows that when shooting this close and tight, you can create an air of mystery by dirtying the frame briefly. This can be achieved by having the other actor move his hand, or some other object, into the frame. It will be so out of focus, we won't know what we're seeing, but we'll try to look through the blurring to see who's beyond.

The fourth frame shows that if you're shooting an extreme close-up of somebody wearing sunglasses, you have to do something inventive with the reflection in those glasses to make it worthwhile. We can't see his eye, and although he can convey something through his head movements, the shot would be quite flat if we weren't able to see the poker game reflected in the sunglasses. The beauty of this particular close-up is that it enables us to see a wide shot of the room, and thus the game, without cutting to a wide shot, meaning we stay with a sequence of close-ups.

Extreme close-ups should be used only when there is extreme tension, concentration, or when people are waiting for something to happen. They are used to make us wonder what a character is thinking, and rarely work well if the characters are talking.

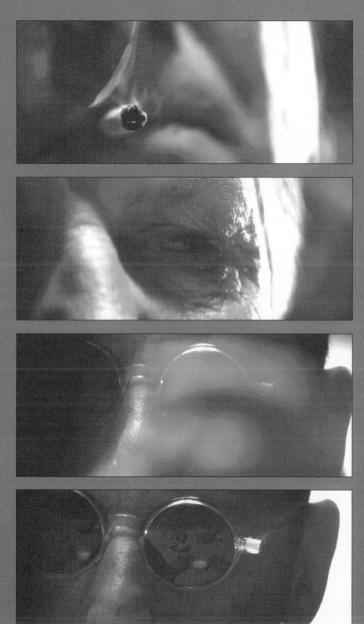

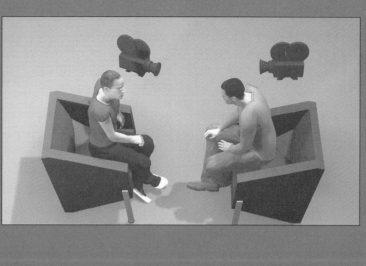

Léon: The Professional. Directed by Luc Besson. Columbia Pictures/Gaumont Film Company, 1994.

ANGLED TALK

When actors talk, you want to see their faces, but setting up good dialogue shots is a challenge. So much so that *Master Shots Vol 2* is dedicated entirely to shooting dialogue scenes. In a chapter on performance, however, it is worth looking at one more way to capture dialogue.

In so many films, the actors stand facing each other and deliver their lines. As an alternative, you can position the actors so that their bodies are both facing one way, which forces them to turn their heads to look at each other. This way, when they do turn their heads, it makes a big impression. We know they aren't looking at each other casually, but deliberately. It also makes it easy for them to avoid eye contact should the conversation become difficult.

In *Blade Runner,* the two actors sit side by side and turn their heads right around to look at each other. They are framed hard to the side of the screen. Even though they are looking directly at each other, we get the feeling that this is a strain, an effort, something they'd rather not be doing. When you use this setup, make sure you put a decent distance between the actors, otherwise it seems discomforting for them to make direct eye contact.

The frames from *Never Let Me Go* show a creative way to position the actors' bodies in the same direction. Rather than sitting on the seat normally, both are turned toward the distant ocean. The choice to position them alongside each other, rather than facing each other, turns a conventional sequence of over-the-shoulder shots into something much more dreamy and remote.

You can break away from a moment like this, and have the characters turn to each other directly, but be aware that this will change the feeling of the scene dramatically.

Blade Runner. Directed by Ridley Scott. Warner Bros. Pictures, 1982.

Never Let Me Go. Directed by Mark Romanek. Fox Searchlight Pictures, 2010.

SLIDE INTO SCENE

How you introduce characters to a scene can have a great effect on the performance that follows. Actors rarely like just walking up to their marks and saying their lines. If you can create a shot that moves everybody into place with some visual style, it can give the actors more confidence in their performance, and gives the audience something more interesting to look at.

This scene from *Laurel Canyon* ends up with the two actors delivering their lines in a conventional set of over-the-shoulder reverses. This works because the introduction to the scene is so full of motion, and we feel like we're watching a lively, well-blocked scene, rather than two actors standing still and exchanging lines.

The move is a dolly from left to right, but it is motivated by the movement of three actors. The first rushes past frame, close to camera. The second emerges in the background (drinking from a bottle) and we follow him for a beat, and then by the third frame, Alessandro Nivola enters the shot and we follow him.

If Alessandro Nivola had entered the room alone and we'd followed him to his mark, it would feel artificial, but because several people are moving into the room, we get a sense of everybody arriving from somewhere else, and it makes sense for him to move in and then stop when he sees Kate Beckinsale.

This shot is over in a couple of seconds, but the rush of movement in those opening seconds is a clever way of starting the scene with a sense of action, and getting the actor into position. Throughout the scene, a small amount of background action maintains this sense of movement in the room. Without that, the opening could feel contrived.

When you're about to show a dialogue scene, and you're putting two actors together, especially if it's the first time they've talked, find a strong visual way to get them together. Using lots of motion across a room is one way to achieve this without anything more complex than a brief dolly.

OWNING A SCENE

When you're featuring a powerful character, especially a frightening character, you need to give the actor the chance to own the scene. This means that he dominates the other characters, but he also dominates the frame itself. There are many ways to achieve this, but these two scenes from *Léon: The Professional* show easy approaches to staging shots that have a strong impact.

In the first, Gary Oldman, who hasn't yet been seen in the film, has his back to the camera. When another character approaches him and we expect him to turn, he delays his turn by removing his headphones. Finally, after an excruciating delay, he turns, but even then he doesn't turn all the way around. This makes us, the audience, feel insignificant to him, and creates a strong feeling that we're dealing with somebody powerful, immovable, and frightening.

In the next scene, Oldman literally dominates the frame, even when he's in the background, by throwing his arms out. It's as though the character refuses to appear small in the frame. He then strides up to the camera.

The final frame is shot from below, which creates the sensation that we're pushing Michael Badalucco up against the wall, which is exactly what Oldman's charater is doing. Also, you can see Oldman's arm rise into the shot. Even in a tight close-up, the character is refusing to be left out of the frame.

When shooting extremely powerful characters, it's helpful to think of them as dominating every moment, of being everpresent, and trying to loom large in every shot.

Léon: The Professional. Directed by Luc Besson. Columbia Pictures/Gaumont Film Company, 1994.

PARALLEL SPACE

Sometimes you can get the best performances when you put both actors in the same frame, rather than giving each a close-up. Some actors prefer their own close-up, but others will enjoy creating a shot where it's the interplay of the characters that creates the effect.

A shot such as this one from *The Book of Eli* shows that even when you're using a fairly long lens, which causes one character to be out of focus, you can get a strong sense of the relationship between people if you don't cut, but let the scene unfold in one take.

In the opening frame, Oldman is in profile. You could shoot this in many ways, according to the story, and in this case the setup makes him appear inscrutable. He's revealing unpleasant information, and if he has any feelings, he's hiding them.

In the background, although Jennifer Beals is out of focus, we observe her reaction, and see her come up to him. As she moves into place beside him, there is a short push in from the dolly. This is optional, and the scene could work without it, but it serves to underline her movement.

Rather than positioning herself in profile as well, her face is directly toward the camera. This is because she is the opposite of inscrutable; we can see everything that she's thinking and feeling, so we're looking straight at her. The setup also works because their faces are so close. In this moment of conflict, their faces almost appear to be touching, which makes it heart-wrenching and painful to watch.

Finally, he turns away from her, revealing more of his expression to us, as she clings to him. With almost no camera move, we get to see the brutal relationship between these two played out. When shooting moments of conflict between two characters, consider putting them in the same frame, and letting their movement in relationship to each other dictate the mood and meaning of the shot.

The Book of Eli. Directed by the Hughes Brothers. Summit Entertainment, 2010.

SEPARATING CHARACTERS

When you show a connection between characters after they have physically parted, you send a strong emotional message to the audience. You make it clear that the characters are thinking about each other, and considering their feelings for each other.

These frames from *Love Actually* show Hugh Grant completing a conversation with Martine McCutcheon and then walking away. We follow him down the corridor, his back to us the whole time, with Nina Sosanya visible ahead of him. It's important to have Sosanya in the frame, because when Grant stops walking, the camera stops, and she continues walking away. This combination of him stopping, the camera stopping, and her continuing on, puts a great emphasis on the fact that he has stopped.

When he turns, he doesn't turn all the way around, but far enough to justify a cut to McCutcheon. This is shot with a long lens, and she is placed in the center of the frame to show that he is looking directly at her. Putting her so central could lead to an unbalanced shot, so background actors help to lessen this effect slightly.

The previous shot of Grant was almost a close-up, but the director now switches to a relatively wide shot. The camera remains in place and Grant walks away. If we followed him again, it would signify that he was moving on from this moment. By leaving the camera where it is, and having him walk away, it feels as though this moment is lingering and will not be forgotten.

When you show a connection between characters, especially over a distance, bringing the camera to rest as they move on can indicate that emotion is going to linger.

Love Actually. Directed by Richard Curtis. Universal Pictures, 2003.

CHAPTER 9

CAMERA HEIGHT

HEAD HEIGHTS

The height of your camera has a substantial effect on your shot. Sometimes, it can be the main factor that contributes to a shot's effectiveness. Despite this, many directors keep the camera at head height for every scene, whatever's happening, which leads to films that are visually lackluster.

For some shots, however, you want the camera to be at head height, but when you do, there are small changes you can make that improve their quality.

In these two frames from *Hard Candy,* you can see that the camera is apparently at the head height of both actors. In fact, it is a bit lower than their heads, and is looking up slightly. Also, the eyes are framed slightly higher in the shot than is standard. These adjustments to standard framing create a sense of claustrophobia within this scene, and almost make us feel overly intimate with the characters.

In the three frames from *Inception,* the director shoots Ellen Page at head height. Whether the camera is behind Leonardo DiCaprio or closer to her, it remains at her head height. We aren't looking down at her, but because she is looking up at him, we sense that she is being admonished.

The shot of DiCaprio is taken from approximately her head height. This means that we focus on her emotions during the scene, more than his. We are with her when we're looking at her, and when we're looking at him, so our concern is with how she will respond to the situation.

This shows how camera height can guide the audience's attention and sympathies, and suggests that you should never put the camera at an unusual height simply to look good. Camera height has a profound effect on shots, and should be considered carefully, whether it is conventional or not.

ANGLE INTRUSION

Low camera angles work especially well when the camera is canted over. The sensation created by this effect can be seen in the first frame from *Léon: The Professional.* All we're looking at is a man standing in an elevator, but imagine how different this would be if the camera was level and at head height. Because it is low, and canted over, we get the sense that trouble is on the way.

Without moving the camera, you can use this low angle to let other objects intrude into the frame. The character on the left raises his gun into frame. A second later, the other character raises his gun into frame.

The effect of this angle, and this brief sequence of moves, is to create great tension and reveal a major story detail — these two men are about to get into a gunfight. This is all achieved in a tight space, with no camera moves or cuts.

Although seemingly simple, shots like this require great cooperation from your actors. To get those guns into exactly the right place in frame will take a lot of adjustment and practice. The actors may feel they are putting their hands into an artificially outstretched place, or somewhere that doesn't feel natural. You need to convince your actors that, because of the unusual angle, their movements will look realistic.

Due to the technical nature of a shot like this, rehearse at low speed a few times, to ensure focus and placement is correct. It's better to get the technical aspects right before the actors burn out.

Léon: The Professional. Directed by Luc Besson. Columbia Pictures/Gaumont Film Company, 1994.

ANGLED HEIGHTS

When you want to emphasize the power imbalance between two characters, you can put them at different heights. To make the effect even clearer, you can adjust the camera to amplify the height difference.

In these frames from *The Karate Kid* there is an obvious height difference between Jackie Chan and Jaden Smith. The director could have Chan stand up straight to create a greater height difference, but this would move their faces too far apart. Instead, Chan leans down and brings his face low. This reduces the physical height difference between them, so in each shot the camera must be moved. When shooting Chan, the camera is taken much lower than Smith's head height. When shooting Smith, the camera is higher than Chan's head.

This small change in height, just above and below the actors' eyes, reflects the struggle going on between the characters. If the camera was level for each shot, or if Chan was standing, the effect would be lost.

In *Derailed,* Clive Owen is left sitting, so that his look-up to Sandra Bee is highly exaggerated. Again, the camera is placed above her head, to gaze right down at him. When we see her, the camera is below his eyeline. It's the same setup as in *The Karate Kid,* but because Owen is seated while Bee is standing, the effect is much more extreme.

The Karate Kid. Directed by Harald Zwart. Columbia Pictures, 2010.

Derailed. Directed by Mikael Håfström. The Weinstein Company (US), Buena Vista International (Non-US), 2005.

DOWN TO CAMERA

In some scenes, one character is tense, while the other remains calm. You can use camera height to show this difference. When the characters move into the same frame, you symbolize that they have reached a joint decision, or overcome the tension.

In *Heavenly Creatures,* Kate Winslet is shot with a low camera. She is on the other side of the room, so we feel how low the camera is, and her pacing makes her appear extremely tense.

The shot of Melanie Lynskey is also taken from a low angle, but because she is closer to the camera, and sitting down, we don't feel tension from her. This matches her dialogue.

Winslet then moves toward Lynskey to join her. This shot is taken from a camera that's at their level, rather than looking up at them, to symbolize that things have normalized for them. They are now at the same height, in a frame that feels more like a normal shot. Even though they are facing away from each other, it feels as though a decision has been made, and the tension overcome.

If this third shot was taken from the same low angle, we would not feel the same sense of calm connection. The low angle would make it feel as though the tension was continuing despite their physical proximity.

This change in camera height and distance is quite minimal, and should make you aware that camera height should never be arbitrary. Whatever your setup, you should check that camera height isn't affecting the meaning unintentionally.

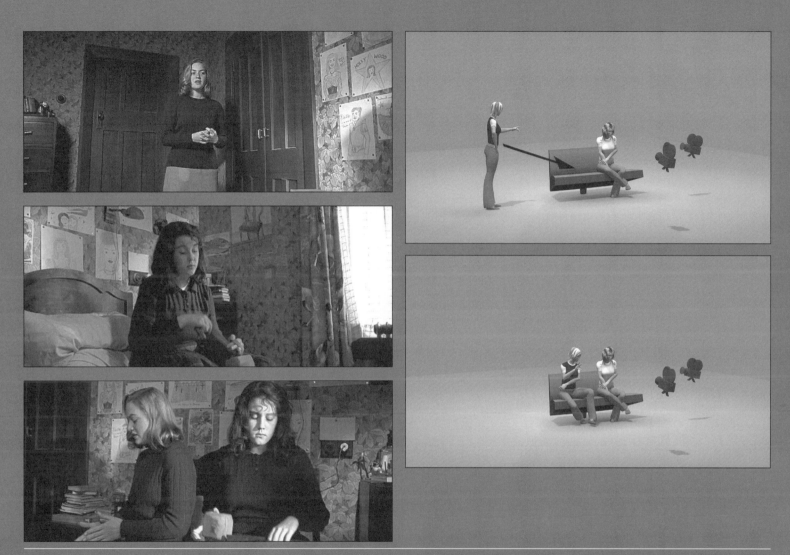

Heavenly Creatures. Directed by Peter Jackson. Miramax Films, 1994.

FLATTENING THE SHOT

Having the camera move from above your characters until it is on their level can create a sense that the action has settled for a moment. You can use this to bring an action sequence to a conclusion, or to misdirect the audience into feeling that all is well when action is about to burst in on the characters.

In these frames from *Harry Potter and the Deathly Hallows: Part 1*, three characters have been arranged in a triangle. This means that the camera pointing toward Daniel Radcliffe will feature him even as it is lowered down; he will remain in view between the other two actors.

The camera that's pointed toward Emma Watson and Rupert Grint will keep them in frame through the downward move as well. This triangular arrangement is common when using groups of three actors.

To shoot the whole scene at head height would make this feel like any other conversation, but starting high and then craning down creates the feeling of settling. Although the dialogue may be full of concern, we feel that this is a pause in the proceedings.

The flattening move, which feels calming, is the perfect misdirection for introducing villains in the background. In the third frame you can see that two characters have been subtly revealed in the background. These characters are about to attack this group of three, so their appearance is important. If you don't show them at all, having them burst into the scene might feel too abrupt, but featuring them directly would be too obvious.

As shown in the overhead diagram, this works when the camera moves straight down, but you can push in slightly as well, as shown in *Harry Potter.* As with most of the shots in this book, you can get the effect you want even when working handheld. Crane shots require practice if you're to get them to work handheld, but so long as the rest of the scene is handheld, they can cut in quite unobtrusively.

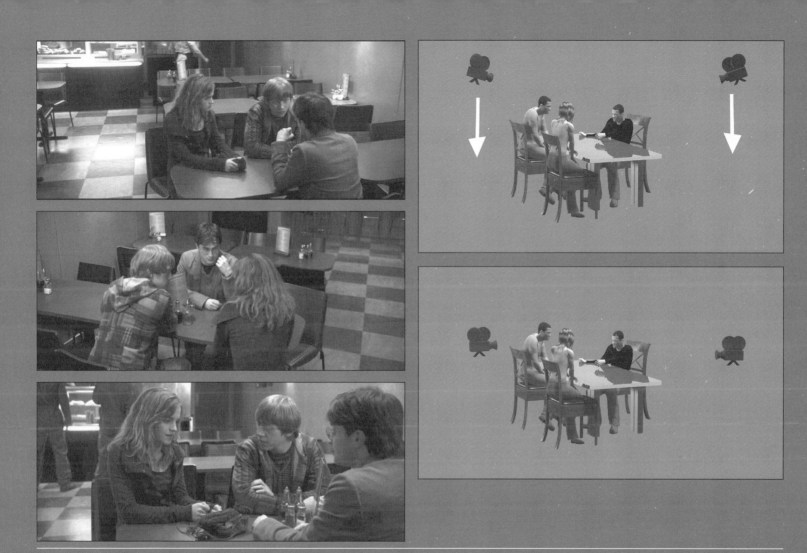

Harry Potter and the Deathly Hallows: Part 1. Directed by David Yates. Warner Bros. Pictures, 2010.

HIGH ANGLE

Before you raise your camera higher than you can hold it, ensure you look to safety first. It's never worth hanging off the side of a building to get a shot, when the results can be disastrous. When you can get a handle on the safety issues, getting yourself above head height yields fantastic results.

The first three frames from *The Karate Kid* show a combination of moves and effects that create a great feeling of motion, even though the camera is a long way from the actors. By placing the camera so high up, we are able to see all of the actors rushing through the scene, which generates both pace and a reminder that there are several pursuers.

If you look at the frames closely, you can see that the camera dollies from left to right, just a few feet, keeping pace with the actors running below. It is not aligned with the street going from the left to the right of frame, which would be a much less impressive shot; instead, the street crosses the frame at a slight angle. Also, as the camera moves, it is wobbled slightly as though handheld, even though it is clearly secured on a crane/dolly arrangement over the edge of the building.

If you have no way of organizing the correct equipment, you still may find opportunities to shoot similar shots, through large glass windows in tall buildings, for example. Rather than thinking a shot is impossible due to limitations, look for ways it can be adapted to suit your circumstances.

The second shot uses a camera placed above head height, with a short lens. As Jaden Smith runs past, the camera pans to keep him in frame. This is easy to achieve, but the combination of such a fast move, with a short lens, creates a rush of distortion around the actor, giving a sense of speed.

The Karate Kid. Directed by Harald Zwart. Columbia Pictures, 2010. All rights reserved.

MOTIONLESS LOOK-UP

Placing the camera on the ground is one way to get a different perspective on a scene, and it can add unexpected drama to dialogue scenes.

In this shot from *Harry Potter and the Deathly Hallows: Part 1*, the camera is placed almost on the floor, and the actors are filmed having a conversation in the far distance. A long lens means that anybody who passes close to the camera remains out of focus, helping us to feel the distance between the actors and the camera. Also, by being so low, we are able to see the ceiling lights, which also help convey distance. If you use this sort of shot, ensure that there are markers to reveal distance to the viewer, or when the actors walk toward the camera, it can feel like they are hardly moving at all.

The second frame shows that when the actors get closer, we are able to see all their faces as they continue the dialogue. As well as sensing the urgency of their predicament from their speed-walk, we get to see all three faces at once, capturing everybody's emotions. This is a good technique when shooting a group of people facing a dramatic dilemma, and is an alternative to cutting from face to face.

The third frame shows that when the actors get closer to camera, it must tilt up to keep them in frame. This gives them a more commanding appearance than they had through the rest of the shot, so time this to coincide with dialogue that matches the visual. This is a good point for a decision to be made, and you can let the camera stop following them, and have the actors walk forward until their faces are out of the shot.

UNSEEN FACE

Camera height is often used to show who has the upper hand in a scene, but it can also be used to conceal information, to make a revelation more dramatic.

In this scene from *The Book of Eli,* the fight is over, and the aggressor, Evan Jones, is now slumped on the floor. Although we've seen Denzel Washington's character many times before this scene, it is in the previous moments that we have seen a new side to him. As such, his face is removed from the scene to create a sense of mystery. The camera is put down at the level of the slumped man. It's important that we see Washington's silhouette here, but not his face. If he was farther back, and absent from the short, that would not create the same mystery as having his face missing from the shot.

In the next frame, the camera is placed slightly above Jones, as he looks up. If the camera was higher than this, it would feel like we were looking down on him, but we need to engage with his sense of wonder. As such, a slight angle down is all that's required.

The framing of Washington is slightly lower than his head, looking up slightly, as he looks down. This is the first time we've seen his face for a couple of shots, and because his face has been hidden until now, we are fascinated to see what he's thinking. A lower camera or wider lens would make his face too small in the screen. A closer shot would be too abrupt a change from the shot of Jones.

When a character reveals a new side of himself, consider using camera height to conceal his face for a few beats, and you create a sense of mystery that hooks the audience.

The Book of Eli. Directed by the Hughes brothers. Warner Bros. Pictures (US) Summit Entertainment (Int), 2010.

LOW SLIDE

It's rare for directors to combine a low camera with a dolly move. A push in from a low angle can seem contrived. However, when the camera dollies across the main lines of action, and pans to follow a character through the scene, it gives that character the impression of majesty and power.

This scene from *X-Men: The Last Stand* begins with Ian McKellen framed centrally, from a low camera. As he walks forward, the camera pans around to follow him, but it does this slowly. The slow push prevents the camera getting so close that he obliterates the frame.

As he moves further into the room, the pan puts him to the left of frame, as the dolly across the room continues. McKellen then turns, almost in an arc, and moves back toward the camera slightly. This move can be achieved on the spot, but works well if there is an arc to the movement.

The closing frame of this shot is remarkably similar to the opening frame, which is why this looks so good. He's made a dramatic entrance, then walks calmly forward to make a speech, and all eyes remain glued on him, just as they were when he entered.

The low camera also makes the most of this particular location, due to the high ceilings and large stained-glass windows. It might not work as effectively if the ceiling was featureless, but it could easily work outside.

SEATED POWER

Camera height can be used to show an unexpected reversal of power. In this scene from *Love Actually,* Hugh Grant plays the British prime minister, but instead of conveying his authority, he appears uncertain.

He's sitting behind a desk, framed centrally, but because the camera is looking down at him, and because he's looking up at Martine McCutcheon, he appears nervous.

When we cut to the reverse of McCutcheon, the camera is at Grant's head height, but off to one side. As she approaches, the camera tilts up to keep her in the frame, and this makes us feel how low the camera is. The contrast between the two shots is marked.

Although this is a light scene, used to convey sexual attraction, it's important for us to feel that Grant's character is the underdog, for us to sympathize with him. This is not a scene in which McCutcheon has power over him, but one in which she makes him feel slightly out of control despite her bright nature. The simple camera work reflects this effortlessly.

A similar setup is seen in *Never Let Me Go,* although it is more subtle, because the sensation of power imbalance is meant to be more subtle. The camera that's facing the teacher, Sally Hawkins, is almost on her level. The camera facing Izzy Meikle-Small looks up at her, but only slightly.

The smallest changes to height and angle can have a large impact on the result. The audience will almost never notice these changes consciously, but the mood and meaning of a scene can be governed by camera height, and it should always be considered before you roll.

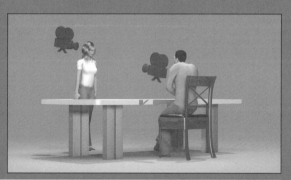

COMPLEX SPIN

When creating complex moves, your aim is not to look impressive, but to convey as much visual information as you can, clearly, and without cutting.

This move from *The Fighter* includes creative use of focus as well as a camera move, to direct attention throughout the scene. The viewer will take in the story, but should not notice the effort you've put into your move.

In the opening frame we see Mark Wahlberg (with his back to us), talking to Ross Bickell. When they mention two other characters, the camera pulls focus to the actors in the background. This is a surprising reveal, and is followed by the camera immediately beginning to arc around Wahlberg.

By the time the camera has come to the point where Bickell is centered, focus has been pulled back to him, with Wahlberg visible on the right of frame. As the camera completes its arc around them, Bickell drifts out to frame left, and we are left with a close-up of Wahlberg. This final frame has a tight eyeline, so that we're almost looking into his eyes, and seeing his expression clearly.

By combining focus with an arc, we've seen two characters talking, two others being revealed, and then ended with a close-up of the main character. A move such as this shows us the big picture, and the issues and people that are being considered, but then focuses in on how it affects the hero. Reserve shots as powerful as this for times when your main character is being faced with one of the largest decisions he has to make.

ACTORS IN MOTION

Some complex moves involve quite basic dollies across a room, but it is the movement of the actors that introduces complexity and interest. This can work when there is snappy dialogue, and is particularly powerful when a conversation ends with one character being left alone with her thoughts, as with this shot from *Derailed*.

The overhead diagram shows the overall movement that takes place. The camera pushes forward and to the left, Clive Owen moves through the room and to the left, while Melissa George walks away and leaves. Although this is a good outline, a lot of movement goes on through the scene.

When Owen appears in the shot, he is framed by the door, and has his back partially turned to us. He then moves across the room, and takes up his final position, facing into the room, as the camera continues its slow crawl across the room.

George begins the scene in the mid-ground, moves forward and across the room (with the focus pulling to follow her), and then she moves away to the distant door and out. Focus is used to direct attention, rather than panning; as we dolly across, the angle is barely changed, so it's vital to change focus according to who's dominating the frame.

The dolly move is so slow that we don't notice it, but the scene begins with one framing and ends with a completely different shot. This is a move that enables you to show change taking place, without cutting to lots of setups. It also enables the actors to interact within the frame.

CUTTING FROM THE MASTER

In many complex shots, the director chooses not to cut away from the master, but tries to contain all the action within that shot. You can, however, cut to another character, and still convey all the motion and action of the master shot itself.

These frames from *Heavenly Creatures* show a basic shot of Melanie Lynskey, combined with a moving master shot. Once it's been established that Lynskey is sitting down, listening to music play, we cut to Chris Clarkson, who is watching her. From behind him, Simon O'Connor appears, moving forward. The camera moves back, faster than he moves forward, to make room for him.

This backward motion cleverly reframes the entire shot, so that Clarkson is now a mid-ground observer, with another character observing from the far background.

We cut back to Lynskey to see her reaction to being mocked, and then she gets up and moves into the master shot (attempting to grab the fish). When you watch the whole sequence, it feels like there's continual motion, even though the shots of Lynskey are static.

When designing shots, don't be afraid to cut away to a motionless shot, so long as your character is showing sufficient expression to keep the scene's momentum going.

DIAGONAL REVEAL

When you track the camera diagonally across a room, and let your actors move through the space in a curve, you give the audience a full sense of the space. This is also a way to give strong visual impact to a scene that could potentially be dull. It's worth noting that the final frame here is the strongest composition. This was probably the first part to be staged, with everybody's marks placed exactly, and the rest of the shot could be designed from there.

The scene opens with the German officers moving through the doorway, and the camera begins its diagonal move to the left. The officers move faster than the dolly, even though they are far away, which moves them from the left to the right of frame.

Also, partway through the shot, a worker moves from the center of the frame to the left (which helps give impetus to the dolly move); his movement makes it feel natural for the camera to keep moving. He becomes framed in the center when the officers complete their arc and join him.

The move itself is a dolly, diagonally away from the door, but the motion of the actors playing the officers, and the arrangement of props, make this visually stunning. When the shot opens we are looking past flames, and when it closes, the wooden boxes fill the lower part of the frame. The shot never lacks visual interest.

On paper, this might be described so simply that an average director would just show the actors walking to their marks. By drifting the camera across the room, and letting the actors navigate the various obstacles, we get to see the entire, elaborate set, and their slow, menacing progress through the scene.

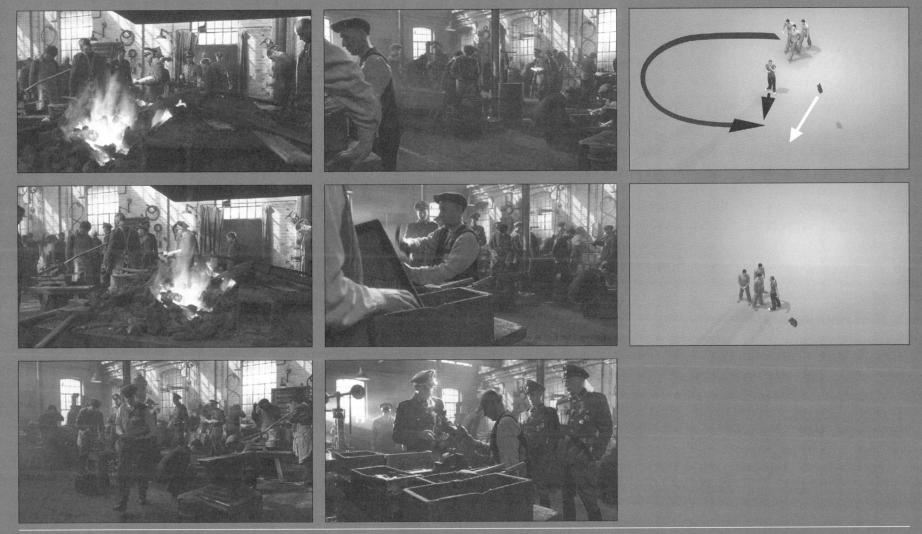

LONG TRACK

Long tracking shots, where we follow the characters through a complex sequence of moves, have been around for decades. Directors tend to show off with them, and this can be irritating. Sometimes they are used with great humor and irony, such as the opening shot of *The Player* (which actually included a disguised cut, and also has dialogue referencing long tracking shots).

These long takes, covering lots of ground, are sometimes designed to boost the director's ego, but that doesn't mean they should always be avoided for the sake of humility. A good tracking shot, well designed, creates a flow of motion and interaction that is exciting to watch. The best tracking shots are those that follow a character who has a good reason to be on the move. They can become quite dull when it's just two people ambling along having a conversation.

This example from *Love Actually* works so well that it's difficult to imagine it being shot any other way. The purpose of the shot is to introduce that we're at 10 Downing Street, and that Hugh Grant is thus the British prime minister, and then follow him into this place of power for the first time. Going behind closed doors is always fun, and it thrills the audience to follow him in there, so doing this in one long take is ideal.

You can achieve tracking shots with a combination of cranes and dolly, but it's more common to use a camera stabilizer to chase after the character. That's exactly what happens here, and although it works well, it does illustrate why you should limit these shots. Camera stabilizers tend to require short to medium lenses, and the operator has to make compromises to ensure that everything stays in shot. As such, the framing is always a little on the ordinary side. It works, because there's a new environment, an exciting moment, and a move into an interesting building. But you wouldn't want to shoot a whole movie in this way, or everything would begin to feel average.

Love Actually. Directed by Richard Curtis. Universal Pictures, 2003.

DOLLY FRAME

Some of the best shots are achieved when something unexpected enters the frame. In *Schindler's List,* what appears to be a walk across the street becomes more interesting when we see a car come into frame.

The camera moves back more slowly than Ben Kingsley walks forward, so that he gets closer to the camera. This conveys his haste, and the camera dolly slows as he approaches the vehicle.

At this point his face would go out of shot, so Spielberg has him lean down to look into the car. This works, because it makes sense for his character to do that, but this is a masterful way of compensating for a potential problem. You can also see that he's strongly lit at this point, to make him show up clearly. Without this, we might have trouble picking out his face through all the motion across the screen.

This in itself would be a masterful shot, but the camera continues its slow journey backward to reveal Liam Neeson, sitting in the driver's seat. At this point, Kingsley moves to get into the car, and focus is pulled onto Neeson.

The dolly move used here is extremely simple, but the creative placement of the car, its sudden appearance in the frame, and the way the characters are framed through and within it make this shot so successful.

When setting up your shots, let the camera start in a place where only part of the scene is revealed, and let your move reveal the destination and other characters as the scene unfolds.

Schindler's List. Directed by Steven Spielberg. Universal Pictures, 1993. All rights reserved.

PUSH TO CLOSE-UP

When you move characters past the camera, you can create a moment of surprise when another character moves into the center of frame. This works especially well if the camera is moving forward and then stops on the character.

This shot from *Léon: The Professional* begins by establishing that the corridor is empty, with distant characters about to enter through the doors. The camera moves forward in a straight track down the corridor, and the actors begin to move into the frame and then past. They are not rushing, but pacing their way down, and the camera progresses steadily.

The feeling this shot produces is one of methodical preparation, but then surprises us by having the villain of the piece, Gary Oldman, walk into frame and move straight into a close-up. His appearance interrupts the steady progress of the camera. It's as though the shot has always been heading to this point, and we experience contradictory feelings; his appearance is a surprise, but also seems inevitable now that it's occurred. This in itself creates fear.

A short lens is used, to make the corridor seem longer, and so that Oldman looms up on us rapidly. Every other character moves to either side of the camera, but he moves directly in front, establishing his menace beyond doubt.

In Chapter 7.5 Push Against Flow, you see the camera push forward as actors rush past. In this shot, from the same film, there is a similar setup, but due to pacing and staging differences, it has a completely different effect. It's worth studying them together, to see how the different effects are achieved, even though the essential setups are quite similar.

Léon: The Professional. Directed by Luc Besson. Gaumont Film Company/Columbia Pictures, 1994. All rights reserved.

10.8

WIDE TO CLOSE

If you can find a way to move from a wide shot to a close-up, without cutting, you can show an entire scene, revealing what the character sees and how the character responds to the situation.

These frames from *Schindler's List* show a masterful use of a long lens, with a dolly move and a pan. The camera begins on Liam Neeson's left, looking across the space over his right shoulder. This is a long lens, so we're quite a way back from Neeson, and he is completely out of focus, as we watch the couple who enter right of frame.

As the camera dollies to the right it pans to follow the couple moving left. This causes Neeson's form to move across until he is on the right of the frame. At that point, we are expecting the couple to emerge from behind his head. Instead of following them, the camera comes to a rest, and pulls focus rapidly, as Neeson's hand rises into shot.

The money he offers is a strong story point, and if the shot had ended there, it would already have been a superb storytelling moment. The lesson to learn from this shot is that even when you think you've shown everything you can from one setup, look for inventive ways to continue the revelations. Instead of cutting to the next character, Spielberg has the character push his face into shot.

A moment later, there's a final reveal as Neeson turns his head to the side, revealing his profile. This works especially well at the end, because each intrusion into the frame is unexpected. When something is unexpected, we take notice.

In the first part of the shot, we follow the couple because the camera follows them, but then our attention is drawn to each story point as it appears in the frame. Find ways to reveal your story by moving from wide to close-up, through a shift of focus.

Schindler's List. Directed by Steven Spielberg. Universal Pictures, 1993. All rights reserved.

OPPOSING SLIDE

At moments of high drama, you can immerse the audience in the scene by using two dolly moves, going in opposite directions.

In the opening part of this scene, Leonard DiCaprio points the gun, and walks to frame left. As he does so the camera dollies to the right, and pans to keep him in roughly the same part of the frame. This is a strong move, because he is going in the opposite direction to the dolly. To make it even stronger, the reverse shot should reflect how this would look from his point of view.

Rather than repeating the motion, Marion Cotillard stands still, as the camera dollies to the right. This moves her to the left of frame, as several other actors stumble into the shot, with Joseph Gordon-Levitt as their captive.

These two shots are over in moments, but they achieve dramatic tension and rapid storytelling. The combination of these moves creates the effect. If the shot of DiCaprio had involved a dolly, but no actor movement, it would create a feeling of suspension. Likewise, if the shot of Cotillard had her walking to frame left, as we dollied right, it would create a feeling of her circling DiCaprio. This differs entirely from what we have here. In this shot, DiCaprio is trying to avoid being trapped, and sees that his attacker has an ace up her sleeve (in the form of his captive associate who's pushed into frame). The camera moves reflect this completely.

This shows how important it is to know what effect you are trying to achieve with your setups, rather than simply moving the camera around to capture action. Each move should be designed to convey how the character feels, or what he sees, and when done precisely, you can put across a range of emotions and a mass of information in a few seconds.

GROUP IN MOTION

When there's strong tension between a group of characters, you can capture their dynamic in one flowing shot. This enables you to see their reactions to one another, not just in their faces, but in the way they move around each other.

In this shot from *Black Swan,* Winona Rider is close to Natalie Portman, and her hand gestures imply that she's intruding on her space. This is a standard over-the-shoulder shot, except that Vincent Cassel can be seen approaching from the background. The actors are arranged in a line, and we see all three during this opening part of the shot.

As Cassel approaches, Portman backs off, and the camera moves away to make space for her. This leaves us, a moment later, with a direct shot of Portman's face, with the other two grouped behind her. This is a good example of how two beautiful frames can be joined by the simplest of moves, rather than a cut.

As the shot continues, with the focus on Portman, Cassel joins her. After a few moments the camera favors Portman, and Cassel is pushed out of the side of shot. The focus is now on Portman again, and our attention is even drawn to the large gestures of the out-of-focus Ryder in the background.

Don't be afraid to let characters drift in and out of the frame, to help direct attention to the main character. Also, remain aware that characters in the background are more visible to us (even when out of focus) if they were present earlier in the shot.

Directors are sometimes wary of shooting group scenes, or interactions between three or more actors, but a little planning and ingenuity can produce results that convey the ideas smoothly.

CHAPTER 11

THE ADVANCED DIRECTOR

DEEP BLOCKING

Whatever your budget, you can fill out your scenes with a depth of detail and motion. Some scenes require stillness, but when you want to create the sense that something is happening, or about to happen, let background motion complement camera motion.

This scene from *Cast Away* shows a director making the most of the tools available to him. They've paid for access to an airport, a plane, and various trucks, so these are all used to texture the scene. Don't be fooled into thinking this only applies when you have money. Plenty of directors with large budgets manage to shoot entire scenes without using the richness of the sets available to them. The techniques seen in this shot could be applied if you were shooting a scene in a quiet diner, for example. It's not about money, but about how you see things.

The opening frame has Hanks in profile. In the background, the plane is almost facing him. In the background, Nick Searcy approaches on frame right. As Hanks moves to the left, the camera goes with him, letting Searcy take over the focus of the shot until the two of them are sitting on the small truck.

At that point the camera changes direction, and begins to move to the right. Normally, a direction change mid-shot is jarring, but a moment later, in the background, a truck crosses from frame left to right. This helps to soften the camera's motion to the right. (It doesn't have to be a truck. It could be a background actor.)

The camera now begins to push forward, which is another direction change. A truck moves from behind the camera, toward the center of the frame, and the camera moves in the same direction as the truck. It's almost as though the camera is following the truck, which makes this direction change feel natural.

As a bonus, this truck fills the gap between the characters. When shooting a two-shot, what to put between the characters plagues directors. Empty space is boring, but anything too interesting will draw attention. Out-of-focus background movement is perfect.

Whether you're shooting a small scene in a room, or a climactic action sequence in a huge landscape, make use of background motion to give depth to your scene, and motivation to your moves.

MOTIVATE THE CAMERA

Some directors are happy to point the camera at whatever part of the scene they want. Partway through a shot, they will swing around to let the camera look at something else. This can work, but it is far from elegant, and draws attention to the camera, which can break your suspension of disbelief. If you want the audience to stay immersed in the story, ensure that your camera moves are driven by action within the frame.

In these two scenes from *War Horse,* motion is used to direct the camera. In the first example, Emily Watson bends down to pick carrots. As she pulls them out of the ground, the camera follows them up. This upward motion gives the camera the motivation to go all the way up to her face. You could just show her digging, and then tilt up to her face, but that would create a slight mental pause for the viewer, while waiting for the camera to settle. As such, it draws attention to the move, rather than the story. By following an object, the audience is guided through the shot.

You need to find a balance between story and camera move. Don't introduce props to a scene purely to motivate a move, unless they suit the character. Here, we'd expect Watson to be digging carrots, so the shot works.

In the second example, a piece of cloth is being untied from the horse by David Kross. As he pulls it free, we pull back to get a good look at it as well. When he stretches it out, the movement of his hand across the frame motivates the camera to begin its move to the right. He then turns, so that his movement matches the camera's movement. Finally, the camera follows his hand down to his pocket before we cut.

A scene such as that requires exacting timing and delicate staging. Actors may be resistant to this, as it can feel overly technical, but you need to let them know this is the best way to capture their performance. Nothing is spoken in this scene, but we see Kross's realization, contemplation, and reaction. Without a camera move, we would barely notice his acting.

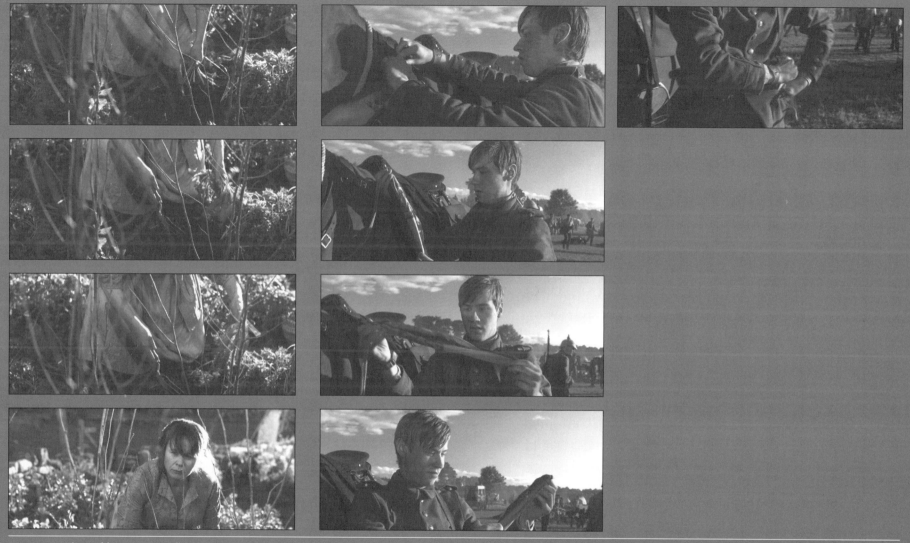

DEVELOPING MOTION

A camera that is in constant motion feels like it is floating around aimlessly, especially if the camera's pace doesn't change. This is why so many long, handheld scenes, which are meant to feel active and interesting, can send viewers to sleep. It feels like a bored documentary crew is wandering around after their subject. Try to change the pace of camera movement within a scene, to keep the viewer interested.

Even in highly expressive scenes, where there's an outburst of emotion, you should try to build in some contrast, to avoid the feeling of the camera drifting through the scene. You can see in the first three frames from *The Fighter* that Christian Bale is initially the main source of movement in the scene. The camera is stationary, while he moves within the frame. Then he turns to face somebody behind the camera and rushes forward as the camera rushes toward him.

The move is so dramatic, and so fast, that it would have felt outrageous if it was tagged on to the end of a scene with no camera movement. Equally, if the camera moved this rapidly throughout the whole scene, the impact of these final moments would be lost.

When planning your shots, be wary of letting the camera drift through the scene. Make sure that actor movement and camera movement are balanced out, to reflect the pace of the story, and the specific scene as it unfolds.

Unusually, the same camera move is recreated moments later. At the very next cut, the camera again pushes in on Bale at great speed (in a different location), ending with his face in a close-up. This has the effect of making us see the character as frantic, but trapped. This is not a technique that should be overused, but it may be worth experimenting with repeated moves, to see what effect they have.

The Fighter. Directed by David O. Russell. The Weinstein Company (Int), Paramount Pictures (US), 2010. All rights reserved.

MAKING USE OF SPACE

When you enter a location or set, your first decisions center on where to stage the action. Beginners tend to gravitate toward the middle of the room. The danger with this is that it can look too similar to the way we see the world on an average day unless you fill the scene with details as shown in these three frames, from *Melancholia.*

John Hurt is framed to the right, even though he's looking to frame right. Normally, you leave a space on the side of the actor's gaze. This framing works though, because he is surrounded by a roomful of people watching him make a speech. The second frame is kept interesting by having Hurt's sleeve introduced in the foreground, with incidental actors passing in the background. The third frame is given depth by having the main actors curve around the center of the frame, with others in the foreground and background. With this much attention to detail, shooting in the middle of the room will not result in a dull shot.

An alternative is to put your character against a wall, as shown in these frames from *The Fighter.* To avoid making the character seem alone, fill the foreground with other actors crossing the frame. This establishes the busy room as the camera pushes in.

To capture the full range of textures in a location, be prepared to get a long way back from your subject, and shoot them moving through the location with an extremely long lens. These frames from *The Adjustment Bureau* show that angle choice is important for this type of shot. If Anthony Mackie was running toward camera, there would be no pan through the shot. If he was running right past camera, the fast pan would blur the background so that we wouldn't get a sense of the space that he's passing through.

You aren't shooting a location; you are shooting a story, but push your characters into interesting parts of the set, and remain aware of the background whenever you shoot.

LOST GEOGRAPHY

When you're shooting scenes with large groups of characters, it takes a great deal of planning and skill to keep the audience focused on the dialogue. Although it may appear as though this scene from *Cast Away* was shot from several angles and then stitched together with tireless editing, it was designed with precision. Every look, every movement, is designed to direct our attention through the flow of the scene.

The scene begins by following a character in to the dinner table, giving us an overview of where everybody is sitting. We don't get to take this all in, but we see Tom Hanks because he moves his arm into the center of frame. Our eye was guided there as the camera came in from the left. His arm is the first thing we see, not least because he is wearing the most distinctive piece of clothing in the scene.

The next frame contains his sleeve once more. As Hanks is not visible in this shot, using his sleeve is a way to orient the audience. Without his reach across the table, we might not be certain whom these other characters were talking to.

We switch across to Hanks' left side, and look across the table, but this is not disorienting, because his face remains in shot. He is the anchor for the whole scene; we know where he's sitting, and so as long as he appears somewhere in frame, we know where we are. This is vital, because if you just edit the conversation together by pointing the camera at the various actors, the audience won't know which way they're facing, or who's talking to whom. They will become confused and irritated by the complexity and will not follow the story.

In the next frame Hanks looks to his left (frame right), because we're about to cut to a shot showing that end of the table. His look motivates that cut, and the audience is guided by his look. Again, a small movement ensures there is no confusion.

Although some new shots are introduced into this lengthy scene, it is constructed mostly from these few shots. The hard work is done in the first few seconds, and then, with the audience confident of who sits where, the scene can be edited according to who speaks.

If you're shooting a large group of characters, use visual cues during the first ten seconds or so to ensure that the audience is absolutely certain of the scene's geography.

Cast Away. Directed by Robert Zemeckis. Twentieth Century Fox (US), DreamWorks (Int), 2000. All rights reserved.

CHARACTER VIEW

There are times when we need to see what a character is looking at. These frames from *Never Let Me Go* show two approaches to this challenge.

In the first, we see somebody walk through a door and the camera pushes in toward the empty doorway. This creates a sense of mystery, and we want to look through the door. The main characters then appear ahead of us, and they too are heading toward the door. As they turn to look through the door, so do we. Importantly, Izzy Meikle-Small remains on the left of shot. We aren't looking through her eyes, but we know we're seeing what she's seeing, because she is looking in that direction.

The second example is the more basic approach, but it uses many small adjustments to make it effective. In the first frame we see the boys on the playing field. A long lens is used, so that the boys are in focus, but the background and foreground are out of focus. This makes them the subject of somebody's gaze.

We now cut to Izzy Meikle-Small and Ella Purnell, who have their heads turned toward the boys. If they were sitting straight on, facing the camera, it might not be so obvious that they are looking at the boys, and might even feel like a cut to another scene. By having them sit at an oblique angle, with their heads turned to look past the camera, their gaze is emphasized.

Finally, Purnell looks away, and Meikle-Small is left staring at the boys. Singling her out in this way makes it clear that this is her scene, and that we're seeing it from her viewpoint.

There are many times when you can show your character, then cut to what she's seeing, and it will make sense. If the subject is secret, or particularly important, it's worth staging your shots to make more of the moment.

STORY POINTS

The best storytellers can work without dialogue, letting the important details of a scene flow together. In this scene from *War Horse,* you can see how all the story points are conveyed, with a minimal number of cuts. If you apply this level of efficiency and flair to your scenes, you can become a powerful storyteller.

In the opening frame we see that the horses are locked away behind the gate, because we look through the gate. With that story point established, the camera moves backward and the gate moves toward camera, opening, and we see that people are entering the field.

In the next frame the camera has been placed at a height so that we see the rope in the man's hand as he walks forward. Another man follows, also carrying a rope, and then the camera has pulled back far enough for us to see the gate being closed and the horses beginning to react.

This shot is nothing more than a dolly back, but tells a clear story: The horses are being approached, and somebody's going to try to harness them against their will.

Two brief shots follow in which we see the rope harness go over the horse's nose. Moments later, the horses are being led away. The camera pushes in as they are led away, adding drama to a shot that might otherwise seem pedestrian.

When trying to convey story points, think of ways you can link them with a combination of camera movement, props, and blocking. The key to getting this right is being absolutely clear about what needs to be seen, and in what order. Once you know that, you can start inventing shots.

War Horse. Directed by Steven Spielberg. DreamWorks Pictures through Touchstone Pictures, 2011.

SCENE STAGING

Long takes give actors the opportunity to create powerful scenes, but you need to match their efforts with camera work that captures performance and reflects the story.

This scene from *There Will Be Blood* feels like one continuous take, but is actually comprised of two shots. Actors can become tired and irritated when they are forced to repeat a long scene time after time, so it's wise to shoot the introduction to the scene separately from the long dialogue section.

The scene opens with movement in the house, and David Willis emerges and heads to frame left. We pan with him until we meet Daniel Day-Lewis and Dillon Freasier. At this point we cut to a shot from another angle. Crucially, the actors remain roughly the same size in the frame at the moment of the cut. This makes the scene feel continuous. Many viewers think they have watched one long take, because the cut is made with the actors appearing the same size in the frame.

The actors now walk up to the house, and the camera gradually crawls toward them, as the dialogue takes place. The family emerges from the house, framed directly between Day-Lewis and Willis. This is symbolic of the issues in the story, and makes us consider the wider implications of the dialogue. Freasier also runs out of frame, briefly, so that we focus more directly on the two men.

As Day-Lewis and Freasier leave, we follow them, but the camera lets them drift to the right of frame. This gives the impression that there is unfinished business here. This is emphasized by the girl running in and joining them for a moment, before they continue on their way.

Long scenes, with no cuts, can be the most memorable part of a film if executed well, but make sure you have a good reason to shoot in this way. If close-ups and tight editing suit the scene better, don't go for a long take just to be impressive. If a long take suits the drawn-out tension of a scene, it's worth finding a way to get the visuals to match the acting.

VISUALIZING THE SCENE

When you're visualizing your scene, think of the viewpoint character. Although the camera will be pointing at your main character throughout the scene, bear in mind that this is her story, and that can help to shape how you shoot.

This scene from *House of Sand and Fog* is an excellent illustration of this approach to filming. Jennifer Connelly is having her house repossessed, so the film is shot to reflect her surprise and unease, and the sense of invasion she feels.

Having her in a dressing gown is an inventive touch that not only shows her as unprepared, but also emphasizes the feeling of vulnerability and domesticity. This contrasts starkly with the official-looking character seen outside her door. Even when she's opened the door, she continues to hide behind it. The background is thrown right out of focus, as though she's trying to conceal the inside of the house from these people.

As Scott N. Stevens pushes in, he dominates the frame, effectively taking over her house. By the time she catches up, we cut to another shot of him. He appears to have moved farther into the house than should be possible in a couple of seconds. This slightly unreal moment underlines Connelly's disorientation.

Connelly is now framed centrally, but there's always somebody in the background, or passing in the foreground, to show that she's effectively surrounded or trapped.

The shot of Stevens leaving also shows a locksmith changing the locks; efficiently revealing a story point and making it feel like everything is happening at an unreal speed. The final shot of Connelly is positioned so that we are almost looking straight into her eyes, to connect with her pain.

By considering your main character's emotional experience of a scene, you will find it easy to contrast a complicated sequence of shots.

House of Sand and Fog. Directed by Vadim Perelman. DreamWorks, 2003. All rights reserved.

CREATING ON-SET

Some directors like to create on-set, just before they shoot. Others like to plan months in advance. Whatever approach you prefer, you will probably find there are times when you have to make up new shots on the spot. Learning to respond quickly and inventively is one of the key skills you need to develop as a director.

When you have to come up with shots at short notice, begin by getting the actors to play out the scene in the most obvious way. Let them position themselves in the scene, and see how it looks. As the scene runs, see where your attention is drawn, and you will begin to get a feeling for what you want to emphasize. Let the actors' creativity feed yours, but if their ideas contradict your overall vision, find a way to guide them back to the film's journey, rather than their own.

This scene from *Melancholia* shows how a scene could be developed in this way. By opening with a close-up on Charlotte Gainsbourg's panic, we engage with the emotion of the scene. The following shot is a series of rapid camera moves back and forth, between her and Kirsten Dunst, until Dunst stands and follows her. This handheld style, with the camera searching for the interest in the scene, does not suit many films. This overall approach, however, of observing the actors to see where the performance shines, can certainly give you a starting point for generating shot ideas.

The two final frames, from *Melancholia,* could have been storyboarded exactly, or it could be that the director came up with these framings once the actors were in place. The truth is probably that a strong vision meshed with a willingness to change.

When planning your scene, imagine clearly. Dream up the best shot that you can, but when you get to set, remember that you are a storyteller. The camera should be used not to capture, but interpret, a scene. Enter every scene with a strong vision, but an open mind.

CONCLUSION

When you read a script, you picture a scene. When you cast your actors, the scene becomes clearer. Once the set is built or the location found, it's impossible to keep your imagination from firing.

Use the knowledge you gain from this book to give intelligence and craft to your inspiration. Aim to make the best movie you can.

Refusing to compromise doesn't mean becoming overly indulgent. I sometimes despair when I see new filmmakers working five hours longer than scheduled to get that perfect shot. If they ever become paid to be directors, that can't happen.

Working to schedule is good practice, and you have to discipline your imagination, so that it can give you the solutions you need without delay. When there's only half an hour left to shoot, you've got to come up with a shot that solves all your problems. You can't wait for perfection.

Armed with the secrets you've gleaned from this book, you will find it easier to create new shots at short notice. When you do that, you become a director that people want to hire, because you can create at speed. Some will call you reliable, others will think you are a genius, but everybody will know that you can be trusted to come up with great shots. Combine that with a little luck, and you may never be out of work.

ABOUT THE AUTHOR

Christopher Kenworthy is the creator of a new series of *Master Shots* e-books (with HD video and audio) including *Master Shots: Action*, *Master Shots: Suspense*, and *Master Shots: Story*. He has worked as a writer, director, and producer for the past thirteen years. He directed *The Sculptor's Ritual*, which played to sold-out screenings in Australia and received strong reviews. Christopher works on music videos, visual effects tutorials, and commercial projects. He's the author of the best-selling *Master Shots Vol 1* and *Master Shots Vol 2*, with *Master Shots Vol 3: The Director's Vision* released in 2013. He's the author of two novels and many short stories. Born in England, he currently lives in Australia with two daughters and the actor Molly Kerr.

www.christopherkenworthy.com
www.thesculptorsritual.com
ck@christopherkenworthy.com

MASTER SHOTS VOL 1 - 2ND ED.
100 ADVANCED CAMERA TECHNIQUES TO GET AN EXPENSIVE LOOK ON YOUR LOW-BUDGET MOVIE

CHRISTOPHER KENWORTHY

BEST SELLER

Master Shots gives filmmakers the techniques they need to execute complex, original shots on any budget. By using powerful master shots and well-executed moves, directors can develop a strong style and stand out from the crowd. Most low-budget movies look low-budget, because the director is forced to compromise at the last minute. *Master Shots* gives you so many powerful techniques that you'll be able to respond, even under pressure, and create knock-out shots. Even when the clock is ticking and the light is fading, the techniques in this book can rescue your film, and make every shot look like it cost a fortune.

Each technique is illustrated with samples from great feature films and computer-generated diagrams for absolute clarity.

"The camera is just a tool, and anyone who thinks making a movie is about knowing how to use a camera is destined to fail. In Master Shots, Christopher Kenworthy offers an excellent manual for using this tool to create images that arouse emotional impact and draw the viewer into the story. No matter what camera you're using, don't even think about turning it on until you've read this book!"

— Catherine Clinch, publisher
  MomsDigitalWorld.com

"Though one needs to choose any addition to a film book library carefully, what with the current plethora of volumes on cinema, Master Shots is an essential addition to any worthwhile collection."

— Scott Essman, publisher,
  Directed By magazine

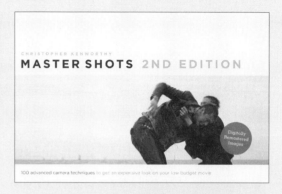

CHRISTOPHER KENWORTHY has worked as a writer, director, and producer for the past ten years. He directed the feature film *The Sculptor*, which played to sold-out screenings in Australia and received strong reviews. Recent works include sketch comedy for the BBC's *Scallywagga*, a title sequence for National Geographic Channel, visual effects for 3D World, music videos for Pieces of Eight Records and Elefant Records, and an animated wall projection for The Blue Room Theatre in Perth, Australia. Kenworthy is the author of the best-selling *Master Shots*, two novels: *The Winter Inside* and *The Quality of Light*, and many short stories. Current projects include screenwriting, several directing assignments, and the development of additional *Master Shots* applications.

$26.95 | 362 PAGES | ORDER NUMBER 179RLS | ISBN: 9781615930876

24 HOURS | 1.800.833.5738 | WWW.MWP.COM

MASTER SHOTS VOL 2
100 WAYS TO SHOOT GREAT DIALOGUE SCENES

CHRISTOPHER KENWORTHY

Building on the success of the best-selling *Master Shots*, this book goes much deeper, revealing the great directors' secrets for making the most of the visual during the usual static dialogue scene. A strong scene is determined from where you put the camera and how you position and direct your actors. This is especially true when shooting dialogue. The techniques in *Master Shots, Vol. 2* ensure that every plot point, every emotion, and every subtle meaning is communicated clearly.

This is the first book to show how important it is to shoot dialogue well. What's the point of opening your scene with a great camera move, if you then just shoot the actors like a couple of talking heads? *Master Shots, Vol. 2* gives you control of dialogue scenes, whether you're shooting two characters or a room filled with multiple conversations.

Using examples from well-known films, the book gives 100 techniques, lavishly illustrated with movie frame-grabs, and overhead diagrams, to show exactly what you need to get the required result. At all times, the techniques have been broken down to their core points, so they will work on a fully equipped Hollywood set, or with the most basic video camera.

"*A terrific sequel to the first* Master Shots. *If there's a cool way to move the camera, Kenworthy has explained it to us. I can't wait to get this book into my students' hands.*"

— John Badham, director, *Saturday Night Fever, WarGames*; author, *I'll Be in My Trailer*

"Master Shots, Vol 2 *will inspire every filmmaker to think carefully about placement and movement of actors as seen through the camera lens. This book increases the reader's appreciation for the critical work of the cinematographer and the director as they speak the language of film through images.*"

— Mary J. Schirmer, screenwriter, screenwriting instructor, *www.screenplayers.net*

CHRISTOPHER KENWORTHY has worked as a writer, director, and producer for the past ten years. He directed the feature film *The Sculptor*, which played to sold-out screenings in Australia and received strong reviews. Recent works include sketch comedy for the BBC's *Scallywagga*, a title sequence for National Geographic Channel, visual effects for 3D World, music videos for Pieces of Eight Records and Elefant Records, and an animated wall projection for The Blue Room Theatre in Perth, Australia. Kenworthy is the author of the best-selling *Master Shots*, two novels: *The Winter Inside* and *The Quality of Light*, and many short stories. Current projects include screenwriting, several directing assignments, and the development of additional *Master Shots* applications.

$26.95 | 240 PAGES | ORDER NUMBER 167RLS | ISBN: 9781615930555

CINEMATIC STORYTELLING
THE 100 MOST POWERFUL FILM CONVENTIONS EVERY FILMMAKER MUST KNOW

JENNIFER VAN SIJL

BEST SELLER

How do directors use screen direction to suggest conflict? How do screenwriters exploit film space to show change? How does editing style determine emotional response?

Many first-time writers and directors do not ask these questions. They forego the huge creative resource of the film medium, defaulting to dialog to tell their screen story. Yet most movies are carried by sound and picture. The industry's most successful writers and directors have mastered the cinematic conventions specific to the medium. They have harnessed non-dialog techniques to create some of the most cinematic moments in movie history.

This book is intended to help writers and directors more fully exploit the medium's inherent storytelling devices. It contains 100 non-dialog techniques that have been used by the industry's top writers and directors. From *Metropolis* and *Citizen Kane* to *Dead Man* and *Kill Bill*, the book illustrates — through 500 frame grabs and 75 script excerpts — how the inherent storytelling devices specific to film were exploited.

You will learn:
· How non-dialog film techniques can advance story.

· How master screenwriters exploit cinematic conventions to create powerful scenarios.

"Cinematic Storytelling *scores a direct hit in terms of concise information and perfectly chosen visuals, and it also searches out... and finds... an emotional core that many books of this nature either miss or are afraid of.*"

— Kirsten Sheridan, Director,
Disco Pigs; Co-writer, *In America*

"*Here is a uniquely fresh, accessible, and truly original contribution to the field. Jennifer van Sijll takes her readers in a wholly new direction, integrating aspects of screenwriting with all the film crafts in a way I've never before seen. It is essential reading not only for screenwriters but also for filmmakers of every stripe.*"

— Prof. Richard Walter,
UCLA Screenwriting Chairman

JENNIFER VAN SIJLL has taught film production, film history, and screenwriting. She is currently on the faculty at San Francisco State's Department of Cinema.

$24.95 | 230 PAGES | ORDER NUMBER 35RLS | ISBN: 9781932907056

In a dark time, a light bringer came along, leading the curious and the frustrated to clarity and empowerment. It took the well-guarded secrets out of the hands of the few and made them available to all. It spread a spirit of openness and creative freedom, and built a storehouse of knowledge dedicated to the betterment of the arts.

The essence of the Michael Wiese Productions (MWP) is empowering people who have the burning desire to express themselves creatively. We help them realize their dreams by putting the tools in their hands. We demystify the sometimes secretive worlds of screenwriting, directing, acting, producing, film financing, and other media crafts.

By doing so, we hope to bring forth a realization of 'conscious media' which we define as being positively charged, emphasizing hope and affirming positive values like trust, cooperation, self-empowerment, freedom, and love. Grounded in the deep roots of myth, it aims to be healing both for those who make the art and those who encounter it. It hopes to be transformative for people, opening doors to new possibilities and pulling back veils to reveal hidden worlds.

MWP has built a storehouse of knowledge unequaled in the world, for no other publisher has so many titles on the media arts. Please visit www.mwp.com where you will find many free resources and a 25% discount on our books. Sign up and become part of the wider creative community!

Onward and upward,

Michael Wiese
Publisher/Filmmaker